REFLECTIONS
ON
POLITICAL ECONOMY

PIETRO VERRI

*Translated from the Italian by Barbara McGilvray
in collaboration with Peter D. Groenewegen*

AUGUSTUS M. KELLEY, PUBLISHERS

First published 1986, Department of Economics,
University of Sydney, Sydney Australia (*Reprints
of Economic Classics*, Series 2, Number 4)

© Copyright 1986 by P.D. Groenewegen. All rights
reserved.

First U.S. edition (reset) published 1993 by
AUGUSTUS M. KELLEY, PUBLISHERS
Fairfield NJ 07004
*By arrangement with the Department of Economics,
University of Sydney*

Library of Congress Cataloging-in-Publication Data

Verri, Pietro, 1728-1797.
 [Meditazioni sulla economia politica. English]
 Reflections on political economy / Pietro Verri ; translated
from the Italian by Barbara McGilvray in collaboration with
Peter D. Groenewegen. —1st U.S. ed.
  p. cm.
 Translation of: Meditazioni sulla economia politica.
 Originally published: 1st ed. Sydney : University of Sydney,
Dept. of Economics, 1986. (Reprints of Economic Classics,
Series 2 ; no. 4)
 Includes bibliographical references.
 ISBN 0-678-01459-0
 1. Economics. I. McGilvray, Barbara. II. Groenewegen,
Peter D. III. Title
HB157.V5513 1993
330—dc20   92-40962

Manufactured in the United States of America

REFLECTIONS ON POLITICAL ECONOMY

TABLE OF CONTENTS

INTRODUCTION		vii
Pietro Verri and Eighteenth Century Economics		xi
The Writing and Publication of the *Meditazioni* in 1771-1772		xx
Some Specific Reactions to Verri's *Meditazioni*		xxv
Some Comments on the Translation and General Acknowledgements		xxviii
REFLECTIONS ON POLITICAL ECONOMY		1
Preface to the First Livorno edition, 1771		3
Preface to the Sixth Livorno edition, 1772		3
I	Trading in Nations where Money is unknown	5
II	Of Money, and How it Increases Trade	6
III	Of the Growth and Decline of the Wealth of a State	9
IV	First Principles of Trade, and Analysis of Price	14
V	General Principles of Economics	21
VI	Of the Detrimental Distribution of Wealth	22
VII	Of Merchants' and Craftsmen's Guilds	25
VIII	Of the Laws Constraining the Exportation of Commodities from a State	28
IX	Of the Freedom of the Grain Trade	30
X	Of Exclusive Privileges	36
XI	Various Sources of Error in Political Economy	38
XII	Whether the Prices of some Commodities should be Fixed by Law	41
XIII	Of the Value of Money and its Influence on Industry	43
XIV	Of the Interest of Money	47
XV	Of the Means by which the Interest of Money may be Lowered	50
XVI	Of Public Banks	53
XVII	Of Circulation	54
XVIII	Of Coined Metals	58
XIX	Of the Balance of Trade	62

XX	Of the Exchanges	66
XXI	Of Population	67
XXII	Of the Spatial Distribution of People	69
XXIII	Possible Errors in Estimating Population Size	71
XXIV	Division of the People into Classes	73
XXV	Of Colonies and Conquests	77
XXVI	How Industry is Stimulated by Bringing Men Closer Together	77
XXVII	Of Agriculture	79
XXVIII	Some Possible Errors in Estimating the Progress of Agriculture	83
XXIX	Of the Origin of Taxes	85
XXX	Of the Principles Guiding Taxation	87
XXXI	Various Forms of Taxation	95
XXXII	Of the Class of Men Among whom Taxation is Best Distributed	97
XXXIII	On Whether All Taxes Should be Assessed on Landed Property	97
XXXIV	Of Taxes on Commodities	104
XXXV	The Method of Making Useful Tax Reforms	107
XXXVI	Whether Taxation as Such is Useful or Harmful	111
XXXVII	Of the Spirit of Finance and Public Economy	115
XXXVIII	Of the First Incentive to Remedy Disorders	117
XXXIX	The Characteristics of a Minister of Finance	118
XL	The Characteristics of a Minister of Economy	119

INTRODUCTION

INTRODUCTION

Pietro Verri's *Meditazioni sulla economia politica*, first published anonymously in Livorno in 1771, appears here at last in English translation. Its publication initially gained its author considerable success. Reprints, sometimes deservedly called new editions, appeared in Naples, Genoa and Milan in 1771. A Venetian version, generally called the fifth edition, contains many critical annotations by the philosopher and economic writer, Gianrinaldo Carli.[1] A sixth version published in 1772 at Livorno, also called the second Livorno edition gives Verri's alterations largely responding to Carli's criticisms. It also contains some notes, mainly of a mathematical nature, generally attributed to Verri's friend, Paolo Frisi[2] and an appendix on General Henry Lloyd's *An Essay on the Theory of Money*, also published in 1771.[3]

---

[1] Gianrinaldo Carli (1720-1795), Professor of Astronomy at Padua (1744-1753), then member of an initially Austrian government appointed Economic Council in Milan from 1753, President after 1765, till his death. He published numerous works on money and trade, often from a historical perspective, many reprinted in the Custodi collection of Italian economic classics (*Scrittori classici italiani di economia politica*, Parte Moderna, Volumes XIII and XIV). His notes on Verri's *Meditazioni* are included in that collection in Volume XV which reprints the text of Verri's work. Carli was a noted antiquarian and historian. In his entry on Carli in the first edition of Palgrave, *Dictionary of Political Economy*, London, Macmillan, 1894, p. 227, Pantaleoni concludes by noting "He tarnishes his character by his excessive hatred and jealousy of Pietro Verri, the economist." On some aspects of this quarrel, see below, pp. xiii, xxii-xxiii.

[2] Paolo Frisi (1728-1784), mathematician and astronomer who taught mathematics (arithmetic and algebra) at the University of Pisa (1754-64) and at the Palatine school in Milan (1764-1784). His move to Milan allowed him to join Pietro and Alessandro Verri, Beccaria and others in the journal, *Il Caffè* (1764-66) and perhaps gave him a taste for mathematical economics. Such a taste is illustrated in the notes and comment appended to the sixth edition of Verri's *Meditazioni* and generally ascribed to him following Custodi and others. For a discussion of this and Frisi's contribution to mathematical economics, see R.D. Theocharis, *Early Developments in Mathematical Economics*, London, Macmillan, 1961, pp. 27-40, and below, pp. xxvi-xxvii.

[3] General Henry Lloyd (1718-1783), army general, philosopher and economic writer. Although born in Wales, Lloyd had a distinguished army career with the Russians and Austrians in Europe. Generally noted as a writer on military history, (see for example, his entry in the *Dictionary of National Biography*) in actual fact his intellectual interests were far more diverse. He anonymously published *An Essay on the English Constitution* (London, J. Almon, 1770) and *An Essay on the Theory of Money* (London, J. Almon, 1771), the work from which an extract was reprinted in the sixth

Not till 1781 did Verri publish a new version of the text which became the definitive one. This removed many of the additions made by himself to the 1772 Livorno edition in reply to Carli's polemic. It also removed the material on Lloyd's essay and notes attributed to Frisi. This final version was prepared for inclusion in the first collection of Verri's major works published by Giuseppi Marelli in Milan in 1781[4] and subsequently in Paris in 1784, in Milan in 1791, in 'London' (in fact, Piacenza) and Turin, both in 1801, and in Pavia in 1803. In 1804, Pietro Custodi reprinted Verri's *Meditazioni* as part of Verri's economic writings in Volume XV of the modern part of his *Scrittori classici italiani*. In this edition, Custodi attempted to distinguish Verri's various alterations to the text and reproduced Carli's extensive notes to the "fifth edition" in the appropriate places. Custodi also reprinted Frisi's material on Lloyd's *Essay* but not Frisi's notes. Since then the *Meditazioni* have been reprinted in Italian on numerous occasions in selections of Verri's works. Such selections successively appeared in 1818, 1835, 1844, 1852 and 1854. Verri's economics was also reprinted in Series I volume 3 of Ferrara's monumental *Biblioteca dell' economista* published in Turin in 1852. In 1964, the 1781 version of the *Meditazioni* was reprinted in a selection from Verri's economic and philosophical writings, *Del Piacere e del dolore ed altri scritti*, edited by Renzo de Felice for the Feltrinelli library of Italian classics. The present translation has been made from this reprint.[5] There seems as yet to be no variorum

---

edition of Verri's *Meditazioni* in 1772. More importantly in the context of Verri's work, he wrote *Essais philosophiques sur les gouvernements*, the manuscript of which is now held at the Fitzwilliam Museum, Cambridge. Lloyd met and befriended Verri in 1759, introduced him to economic studies and in general, influenced his work. A detailed biography is provided in Franco Venturi, "Le Avventure del Generale Henry Lloyd," *Rivista storica italiana*, 91 (2-3), 1979, pp. 369-433 and see also his "Le 'Meditazioni sulla economia politica' di Pietro Verri," *Rivista storica italiani*, 90 (3), 1978, esp. pp. 532-48.

[4] *Discorsi del Conte Verri ... Idee sull' indole del piacere e del dolore; Sulla felicità e Sulla economia politica*, revised with additions by the author. Milan, G. Marelli, 1781. This selection was subsequently represented as the *Opere filosofiche e d'economia politica del Conte Pietro Verri* in the various reprintings mentioned in the text.

[5] The text of this edition, called simply 'Della economia politica' or 'Sull' economia politica,' is that of the 1781 Milan edition which, as indicated, is the final edition prepared by Verri himself for his 1781 selection of major philosophical and economic works. It therefore omits the more polemical parts of the second Livorno edition inspired by Carli's critical annotations and the material attributed to Frisi. Professor Franco Venturi has warned me the De Felice edition cannot be considered

edition of the *Meditazioni*, which carefully traces the sequential alterations to Verri's text and reproduces all the notes and annotations provided by others.

Verri's book was also translated on a number of occasions. The first French translation appeared in 1773 and was reprinted in 1776 and 1779, Other French translations were published in 1801 and 1823. German translations appeared in 1774 and 1785 and a Dutch translation, with commentary by I. van Thoir, in 1801.[6] The rapid publication of a French translation plus the multilingual proclivities of educated Europe in the eighteenth century probably made an English translation redundant. In any case, none has appeared till now. An English translation after more than two centuries can be justified on the ground that few English speaking economists would now list a reading ability of Italian as part of their qualifications, and of course, by the superb contents of Verri's "reflections" themselves.

As was the case with many eighteenth century economic classics, Verri's work dropped into obscurity during the nineteenth century. Although Adam Smith had a copy of the 1772 Livorno edition of Verri's *Meditazioni* in his library[7] and it is possible to suggest he may have used it in the preparation of the *Wealth of Nations*,[8] he did not feel a need to acknowledge Verri directly as one of the many authorities he used in writing his famous book. J.B. Say, in his introduction to the *Treatise* refers to Verri's *Meditazioni* as the book

---

a scholarly edition, if only because it fails to draw the reader's attention to the alterations Verri successively made to the text of the work. There seems to be a need for a more scholarly edition if full justice is to be done to Verri's interesting work.

[6] Bibliographical details in this and the preceding paragraph derive from Oscar Nuccio's bibliographical note to the re-issue of P. Custodi, *Scrittori classici italiani di economia politica*, Roma, Bizarre, 1966, Parte moderna Vol. XVII, pp. cxlix-cl, clvii-clviii and F. Venturi, "Le 'Meditazioni ...' di Pietro Verri," a major source for a substantial part of this introduction.

[7] See H. Mizuta, *Adam Smith's Library*, Cambridge University Press, 1967, p. 149; and see James Bonar, *A Catalogue of the Library of Adam Smith* reissued Kelley, New York, 1966, p. 190, which clearly indicates that the copy owned by Smith was the "sixth" edition published in Livorno, 1772.

[8] An example is the passage in Adam Smith, *An Inquiry into the Nature and Causes of the Wealth of Nations*, Oxford, at the Clarendon Press, 1976, pp. 497-98 (Book IV, chapter III (c) 15-17) which bears a striking resemblance to Verri's argument in the *Meditazioni*, section III (below, pp. 10-12). The notion of a balance between production and consumption could of course have been quite easily adapted by them both from Quesnay's similar analysis in terms of production and circulation. Cf. Venturi "Le 'Meditazioni'," p. 561.

that "approached nearer than any other writer, before Dr. Smith, to the real laws which regulate the production and consumption of wealth."[9] In the 1820's McCulloch praised Verri for his criticism of the Physiocratic opinions "respecting the superior productiveness of the labour employed in agriculture" and subsequently listed him prominently in his *Literature of Political Economy*.[10] Marx likewise cited Verri favorably as a critic of the Physiocrats and on the subject of money, perhaps because he used that phrase 'universal equivalent' which Marx himself favored.[11] He was briefly noted as one of the Italian forerunners of economic liberalism[12] in Ingram's entry, 'Political Economy' for the Encyclopedia Britannica. Although Schumpeter refers to him in his *History of Economic Analysis*[13] and there were entries on Verri in the first edition of Palgrave and the 1930's *Encyclopaedia of the Social Sciences*,[14] he was considered not important enough for inclusion in the second edition of the latter work, despite his earlier reputation as a major contributor to economic liberalism in the eighteenth century. *The New Palgrave*, does, however, contain an entry on Verri.[15]

The remainder of this introduction looks at some specific aspects

---

[9] J.B. Say, *A Treatise on Political Economy*, reissued New York, Kelley, 1971, pp. xxxvi-xxxvii.

[10] J.R. McCulloch, *Principles of Political Economy*, first edition, 1825, London, John Murray reprint, 1870, p. 35; *The Literature of Political Economy*, LSE Reprint, London, 1938, pp. 26-27 where Verri is described as "the most distinguished of the Italian economists."

[11] See Karl Marx, *Contribution to the Critique of Political Economy*, London, Lawrence and Wishart, 1969, p. 151; *Theories of Surplus Value*, Moscow, Foreign Languages Publishing House, Moscow 1962, pp. 59, 62; *Capital*, Moscow, Foreign Languages Publishing House, 1959, pp. 43, 89, 134, largely repeats the gist of the earlier references.

[12] J.K. Ingram, 'Political Economy,' in *Encyclopaedia Britannica*, ninth edition, Edinburgh, A & C Black, 1885, Volume XXIV, p. 362; reprinted as *History of Political Economy*, Edinburgh, A & C Black, 1888, pp. 74-75. Verri was also mentioned in Cossa's popular *Guide to the Study of Political Economy*, London, Macmillan, 1880, pp. 157-58.

[13] See for example J.A. Schumpeter *History of Economic Analysis*, London, Allen and Unwin, 1959, pp. 178, 187.

[14] That is, Ugo Rabennno, 'Pietro Verri,' in *Dictionary of Political Economy*, edited R.H.I. Palgrave, London, Macmillan, 1899, Volume 3, p. 619; Carlo Pagni, 'Pietro Verri' in *Encyclopaedia of the Social Sciences*, edited E.R.A. Seligman, New York, Macmillan, 1935, Volume 15, pp. 239-40.

[15] *The New Palgrave: A Dictionary of Economics*, edited by John Eatwell, Murray Milgate and Peter Newman, London, The Macmillan Press Ltd., 1987, Vol. 4, p. 807.

of the background to the work reprinted. This commences with a brief biographical sketch of Verri, emphasizing his introduction to and knowledge of contemporary economic studies, as well as factors which induced him to write the *Meditazioni* in 1770. Aspects of the various editions, their reception and their change in content are then briefly considered before providing a discussion of matters in the translation to which attention needs to be drawn.

PIETRO VERRI AND EIGHTEENTH CENTURY ECONOMICS

Pietro Verri was born in the Duchy of Milan in 1728, then under Austrian rule as a result of the 1713 peace settlement which ended the war of Spanish Succession. He lived and worked in Milan the major part of his life, dying there in 1797 when the city was occupied by the French and had become part of the Cisalpine Republic following the Napoleonic conquest of northern Italy.

Pietro Verri was the first born in an established, aristocratic Milanese family, with a tradition of public service in the administration. His father, Gabriele Verri, had close ties with the Viennese Court, held the important office of Vicar of Provision for Milan, and was also a noted lawyer and legal scholar.[16] Pietro received a good education at Milan, Rome, Brera and the College of Nobles at Parma, where one of his teachers, G.B. Roberti, became a life long friend. Having completed his general studies, he returned to Milan in 1749 to study law with his father in preparation for the traditional family career in administration. During 1752-3 he accompanied his father to Varese and Vienna, and at the Hapsburg court obtained the title of Chamberlain. Public administration was however not single-mindedly pursued by Pietro Verri as a career during the 1750's. Two explanations can be provided for this. Firstly, Pietro frequently clashed and eventually broke with his father who wanted to mould his spirited son too much to his own traditional ways of public administration. Secondly, there were the temptations of the "good society" modelled on Paris then developing in Milan. Theater, the salon of the Duchess Serbelloni, with whom Pietro conducted a much frowned-on affair, distracted him from the more serious occupations

---

[16] Gabriele Verri (1696-1782) administrator, student of law and jurisprudence. In 1747 he published a major collection of Milanese statutes. In 1749 he was appointed to the Senate of the Milanese state. For further details see F. Venturi, *Settecento riformatore, Volume 1, 1730-1764,* Turin, Einaudi, 1969, pp. 648-59.

for which his father, and family tradition, had destined him. In short, Verri's twenties were passed in rebellion against his parents and in the frivolities of a Milanese libertine with literary pretensions. In 1759 he toyed with a military career, secured an officer's commission and served with the Austrian army in Bavaria during the Seven Years War. Being a soldier did not provide the escape from boredom he was seeking. It did, however, provide a new friend, General Henry Lloyd. The latter appears to have introduced him to economics and the usefulness of more general investigations into "civil society", making him realize how much of his youth had been wasted. From the beginning of 1760 he decided to turn himself into an enlightened reformer. In preparation, he seriously studied the leading authors of the French enlightenment—Montesquieu, Voltaire, Rousseau, Helvétius—in the Imperial Library in Vienna. As shown more fully below, he then also began serious study of economics. At the end of 1760, he completed the first fruits of his studies, the essay, *Degli elementi del commercio*, though this was not published till some years later.

Verri's intellectual progress advanced further when in the winter of 1761-2 he founded an intellectual society, *Società del Caffè*, also known as the *Accademia dei Pugni*, together with his younger brother Alessandro. Other members included Cesare Beccaria, the mathematician Frisi, the sometimes economic writers Longhi and Lambertenghi, and a number of others (Visconti, Colpani, Franci and Biffi). Apart from the stimulus they provided to Beccaria's magnum opus, *Of Crime and Punishment* published in 1764, the group produced a journal from 1764 to 1766 modelled on the English *Spectator*, and simply called, *Il Caffè*. This drew them to the attention of the Paris intellectuals, and induced a trip to that city by Beccaria and Alessandro Verri in 1766-67. Pietro Verri was, however, the center of this ferment of enlightenment ideas and the years from 1764 to 1771 have been aptly described by Nino Valeri (one of his biographers) as years of "volcanic activity." These years ended, it may be noted, with the publication of *Meditazioni sulla economia politica*, his major economic work translated below in English.[17]

---

[17] This section draws heavily on the following sources: F. Venturi, "Le 'Meditazioni ...' di Pietro Verri"; *Settecento riformatore*; Renzo de Felice, introduction to Pietro Verri, *Del Piacere e del dolore ed altri scritti*; P. Custodi, "Notizie di Pietro Verri" in *Scrittori classici italiani*, Volume XV, pp. v-lxii; Oscar Nuccio, "Pietro Verri," in *Scrittori classici italiani*, Volume XVII, pp. iii-clxxvi; Gianmarco Caspari (editor), *Viaggio a Parigi*

These years of volcanic activity were marked as well by Pietro Verri's entry into the world of economic administration and reform in the Milanese state. His activity in this respect must be seen as part of the reform movement associated with the enlightened despotism so characteristic of the reigns of Maria Theresa and Joseph II of Austria. Verri's desire to become an enlightened reformer inspired both his economic studies and his early economic works, since some of them were specifically designed to draw attention to his new-found skills. His historical analysis of the commerce of Milan, demonstrating the need for reform, secured him appointment on 31 January 1764 as member of a "junta" established to reform the General Tax Farm. Because on this "junta" he had fought unsuccessfully for the abolition of the Farm, he was given a position of considerable responsibility on the "reformed" mixed Tax Farm in September 1765 by way of a consolation prize. In November 1765, Verri joined the Supreme Economic Council under the Presidency of Gianrinaldo Carli, thereby making 1765, as Venturi has put it[18] a rather special year for the Lombardian economic reform movement. In 1767, administration of the mixed Tax Farm was placed under the Economic Council . Verri's zeal for reform of indirect taxation through abolition of the Farm and other liberal economic changes now brought him increasingly on a collision course with its President, Carli, whom Verri began to criticize increasingly as a seeker of power for himself and little else. The enmity between them thus created undoubtedly inspired Carli's critical notes to Verri's *Meditazioni* in 1771. Frustration with the Council's inaction also stimulated Verri's growing interest in political change designed to facilitate the economic reforms he was after. These include his flirtations with enlightened despotism so visible in the concluding sections of the *Meditazioni*.

Verri's further campaign for the reform of indirect taxation needs to be particularly noted, because it took place before publication of

---

e Londra 1766-1767, *Carteggio di Pietro e Alessandro Verri*, Milan, Adelphi, 1980; D.A. Limoli, "Pietro Verri: A Lombard Reformer under Enlightened Absolutism and the French Revolution," *Journal of Central European Affairs*, 1958, pp. 254-80; *Storia di Milano*, Fondazioni Treccani degli Alfieri per la storia di Milano, Milan, 1959, Volume XII, *L'età delle riforme (1706-1796)*, esp. Parts II and III and pp. 600-13, the last of which is totally devoted to Pietro Verri. The quote from Valeri is given in De Felice, p. xvii.

[18] Venturi, *Settecento Riformatore*, p. 697; see also pp. 694-97 for further details of this aspect of Verri's career.

his *Meditazioni*. In 1768 he obtained permission to draft a plan for the elimination of the *regalie*, the duties on tobacco, salt and wine (comparable to the French *gabelle*) which were the most profitable taxes leased to the Farm. When Joseph II visited Milan, Verri urged on him the need for further reforms in the Milanese tax system. In 1770, the Empress Maria Theresa actively considered direct collection of the *regalie* in place of their indirect collection through the General Farm. Subsequently an Imperial Order, dated 6 July 1770, abolished the Farm providing compensation for its participants, including the financier Greppi. This constitutes Verri's major triumph as a reformer under the auspices of the enlightened despotism of the Austrian rulers, hence explaining his laudatory comments on its usefulness to reforms written less than six months later in his *Meditazioni*. Verri continued to labour on economic reforms, in 1774 securing removal of many of the internal tolls and customs duties he criticized in his economic writings, and preparing a major tariff reform in 1786. These reforms and his political experience gradually disillusioned him with the benefits for progress from enlightened absolutism, for which he substituted an increasing faith in the rule of law as the guardian of civil and economic liberty. In many respects, the description of Verri as "the Turgot of the Duchy of Milan" is therefore most appropriate. Their ideas on essential economic reforms were very similar but Verri was perhaps more successful as a reformer than his more famous French contemporary.[19]

Although it would be interesting to look at other aspects of Verri's career as an economic reformer, the relevance of his interest in economics to this part of his life has been sufficiently illustrated. As further background to the *Meditazioni*, a brief survey of his early writings needs to be given. The 1760 *Elementi* was followed in 1762 and 1763 by several other economic works. In 1762, at Lucca, Verri anonymously published a *Dialogo sulle monete fra Fromino e*

---

[19] Francesco Vigano, *Schizzo della storia dell' economia politica in Italia*, cited in *Storia di Milano*, Vol. XII pp. 608 n. 2; other details on Verri's association with reforms, including reform of the tax farm and indirect taxation, are given in this volume, pp. 280-82, 606-8. As pointed out below, Verri's critique of tax farming probably owed its origins to criticisms voiced by Forbonnais and Mirabeau's *Théorie de l'impôt* and it formed an important part of the tax material in Verri's *Reflections* (below, pp. 27 and n. 10, pp. 90-1, 105-6). For a detailed historical treatment of eighteenth century tax farming, see G.T. Mathews, *The Royal General Farms in Eighteenth Century France*, New York, Columbia University Press, 1958.

Simplicio, a tract supportive of the examination of the Milanese coinage problems which his friend Beccaria had discussed in more detail in his *Del disordine e de'rimedi della monete nello stato di Milano nell'anno 1762*. A second work, *Considerazioni sul commercio del Stato di Milano* was completed in 1763, largely to impress the authorities with Verri's abilities as an economist. Although parts of this work were used in the preparation of Verri's history of Milan published in the 1780's, the text itself was not published in full until 1939.[20] During 1763, Verri also anonymously published his essay *Meditazioni sulla felicità* in Livorno. This work is of interest to students of his economics because it provides some of its philosophical background, including his utilitarian perspectives probably derived from Helvétius' writings. Examples include Verri's treatment of wealth and ambition as factors explaining increases in power and strength, the contrast between self interest and duty in explaining motivations for useful actions, and the varied incentive effects from actions with remote and more immediate consequences. Other passages, particularly those on progress towards civilization, remind of the opening section of the *Reflections on political economy* and are illustrations of inspiration probably gained from his study of Rousseau. This essay was one of the first products from the *Accademia dei Pugni*; in 1764 another appeared, namely his *Considerazioni sul lusso*, published in the journal, *Il Caffè*.[21] It takes up a number of the themes developed in the *Reflections*: problems associated with sumptuary laws, the relationship between luxury, greater equality in the distribution of wealth and incentives to produce. These subjects

---

[20] Reprinted in Custodi, *Scrittori classici italiani*, Volume XVI, pp. 279-94; Volume XVII, pp. 323-35. These early monetary works by Beccaria and Verri have been reprinted with an introduction by Alberto Quadrio-Curzio and Roberto Scazzieri (*Sul disordine delle moneta a Milano nel settecento: tre saggi di Cesare Beccaria a Pietro Verri*; Milano, Electa, 1986) of which the useful introduction is particularly recommended. Extracts only of the *Considerazioni sul commercio* were included by Custodi in his collection. See *Scrittori classici italiani*, Volume XVII, pp. 349-68.

[21] See Pietro Verri, *Meditazioni sulla felicità* in Pietro Verri, *Del piacere e del dolore ed altri scritti*, esp. pp. 75-80, 89-90, 97-98; Verri's *Considerazioni sul lusso* is included in Custodi, *Scrittori classici Italiani*, Vol. XVII, pp. 336-48. As F. Venturi, *Settecento riformatore*, pp. 706-7 and n. 2 points out, these works also establish Verri as a 'utilitarian' supporter of the maxim, "the greatest happiness for the greatest number," though Verri in his *Sulla felicità* phrased the matter in an even more egalitarian manner: "la maggiore felicità possible divisa colle maggiore uguaglianza possible" (p. 100). The passages on development are on pp. 115-21 (esp. 118-20) and cf. below p. xxiii and n. 38.

Verri was also to treat in his *Memorie storiche sulla economia pubblica dell stato di Milano*, written during 1768 but not published till after his death.[22] Other economic works were completed during 1764. These include a memorandum on customs and excise reform for presentation and consideration by the Supreme Economic Council and a statistical estimate of the balance of trade for Milan in 1752. The last exercise was repeated the following year for 1762, and the lessons Verri learned from this are clearly indicated in the section on this subject in the *Reflections*. Extracts from this work were also included in his *Memorie storiche* which, as already noted, Verri wrote during 1768.[23] Finally, in 1769 Verri wrote what can be described as the dress rehearsal for the Reflections: his *Riflessioni sulle leggi vincolanti principalmente nel commercio dei grani*, of which the first part is essentially a condensed and therefore less fully developed version of the major principles examined in the *Reflections*, as well as their specific application to the grain trade. The year 1770 saw him once again busily writing on taxation, the fruits of which can be seen both in the final sections of the *Reflections*[24] and in the Imperial Decree of duly 1770 abolishing the Tax Farm.

Apart from revealing the serious preparatory work Verri had completed before writing his major economic essay of 1770, these earlier economic works provide an indication of the sources of economics available to a student in the subject during the 1760's. In stark contrast to his *Reflections*, which provide no citations to other work whatsoever, Verri liberally quoted from or paid homage to previous writers in economics in his early writings. As already

---

[22] Verri, *Considerazioni sul lusso*, esp. 339, 340-41, 346-49; cf. *Reflections*, below pp. 21-3, 36-38, 45, 55, 73, 76; see also Verri, *Memorie storiche*, in Custodi, *Scrittori classici italiani*, Vol. XVII, chapter V esp. pp. 136-39 which incidentally repeats some of the quotations from the authorities on the subject given in the earlier *Considerazioni sul lusso*, pp. 346-48.

[23] *Bilancio del commercio dello Stato di Milano per il 1752* and *Bilancio generale del commercio dello Stato di Milano per il 1762*. Verri discussed the difficulties in compiling such statistical pictures of the balance of trade in his *Reflections*, below section XIX, esp. pp. 62-63.

[24] Examples include the definition of the objective of economic policy, the importance of free trade, the theory of price and the importance of a large reproduction to secure a substantial surplus product available for trade. Nuccio's bibliography to his essay on Verri in *Scrittori classici italiani*, vol. XVIII, pp. cxviii-cxxix also lists for this period a number of works by Verri on financial reforms particularly monetary reform and a memorandum on the rent payments in kind due by tenants under the Lombardian leasehold system.

mentioned, he had been introduced to the study of economics by General Henry Lloyd and after a year he was able to list Forbonnais, Melon, Dutot and David Hume as the more important economic authorities he had studied.[25] In his 1762 dialogue on monetary problems the authorities he cited further increased. Apart from Beccaria's essay on the subject which had inspired this dialogue, Verri mentioned Locke and Newton and work by von Bielfeld, Montesquieu and the Italian economists Davanzati, Montanari, Carli and Genovesi.[26] The preface to the 1768 *Memorie storiche* further

---

[25] In a letter dated 10 December 1760 Verri indicated he had studied Forbonnais, Melon, Dutot and Hume in the Imperial Library in Vienna and that this reading had been sufficient to grasp the basic elements, definitions and causal propositions of the science of political economy. Verri's reading of Hume was not confined to the economic essays; he greatly admired the *History of England* as well, and his own history of Milan has been compared to the historical work of the Scottish philosopher. In a letter dated 6 November 1766, Alessandro Verri wrote Pietro that he thought Hume "Il più buono e semplice uomo del mondo" (the most good and unassuming person in the world). Hume's history is cited in Verri's *Memorie Storiche*, p. 94 as well as his *Discourses*, p. 127; see also below, pp. 43 and n. 17, 49 and n. 24, 60 and n. 30, 82 and n. 43, 100 and n. 58, 108 and n. 66, 109 and n. 68, 112 and n. 71, for what appear to be references to Hume's essays. See also *Storia di Milano*, p. 609 and *Viaggio a Parigi e Londra*, p. 61. Verri greatly admired Forbonnais' work, not only his *Elémens du commerce*, 1754 and his *Principes et observations oeconomiques*, 1767 but also his translations of Charles King's *The British Merchant* and Uztariz's *Theory and Practice of Commerce*. See *Memorie storiche*, pp. 97, 105-7, 123 and also below, *Reflections*, pp. 27 and n. 11, 43 and n. 27, 69 and n. 33, 107 and n. 63. In the same letter which commented on Hume, Alessandro reported that Forbonnais' *Elémens* was not highly regarded in Paris, and that he had been told Forbonnais was "a terrible pessimist, always despondent and a person definitely to be avoided." See also F. Venturi, *Settecento riformatore*, pp. 667-71.

[26] Locke and Newton are mentioned as coinage reformers in Verri's *Dialogo*, p. 282, and Locke's *Considerations* (1691) are cited in the *Memorie Storiche*, p. 164 on the proposition that all taxes fall ultimately on the land, a position discussed in the *Reflections* (below, pp. 96-98 and n.56). Jacob Friedrich von Bielfeld (1717-70), a special advisor to Frederick II of Prussia, had written a book, *Institutions politiques* which covered many economic subjects from a practical policy perspective. Verri referred to this on several occasions (e.g. *Dialogo*, p. 290 and cf. *Reflections*, below p.107 n.63). Montesquieu is one of the more frequently cited authors by Verri, not only his *Esprit des Lois*, but also the earlier *Lettres persanes* and *Considérations sur les causes de la grandeur des Romains et de leur décadence*. See *Reflections*, below, pp. 23 n.8, 100 n. 58.

The four Italian economists, of whom two were contemporary and known to Verri, were the most frequently cited by the Milanese school. See F. Venturi, *Settecento riformatore*, pp. 685-88 who also explains the Verri reference to Pagnini, Tavanti and Neri. For Carli, see note 1, p. vii above. Genovesi's work used by Verri included not

expanded on the list of economic authorities cited. It includes Gresham with Locke and Hume as a major British authority, adds Vauban and Savary to the French writers already mentioned and Ulloa to the Spanish authors on political economy. The list of Italian economists with whom he was familiar is expanded by the Tuscan writers Pagnini, Tavanti and Neri. In addition, in the text of this work, Verri made reference to the English writings of Bacon, Culpeper, Davenant, Law and Mandeville, invariably in French translation, and to the French works by Dupré de Saint Maur on money and Mirabeau on taxation.[27] Finally, and perhaps most importantly, in his 1769 *Riflessioni sulle leggi vincolanti*, Verri cited Cantillon, Wallace and Boisguilbert, and the English essays on trade of Cary, Decker and Nickolls. More specifically on the corn trade, Verri cited nearly every important French work which appeared on the subject between 1763 and 1768 and in particular drew heavily on Herbert's famous essay on the "police des grains."[28] In short, by the

---

only his translation of Cary (*Storia del Commercio del Gran-Bretagna*, Napoli 1757) but also his *Lezioni*, of which he apparently was sent a complimentary copy by Genovesi when the first volume was published (see letter to Alessandro Verri, dated 29 April 1767, in *Viaggio a Parigi e Londra*, p. 144). For possible references to Genovesi's work in the *Reflections*, see below, pp. 27 and n.11, 64 and n.33, 107 and n.63.

[27] See *Memorie storiche*, pp. 158, 185, 112, 151, 174, 139, 45, 83, and 137 respectively. The Davenant was cited at second hand, the Culpeper from the edition with Child; Mirabeau's *Théorie de l'impôt* potentially appears to have been a frequent reference in the *Reflections* (below, pp. 82 n.43, 106 n.62), while the citation of Mandeville is interesting in the context of another reference in the *Reflections* (pp. 72-3 n.38) where Verri refers to a "distinguished writer who observes 'that not all political vices are moral vices, nor all moral vices political ones'."

[28] See *Riflessioni*, pp. 398 n.65, 306, 339, 305, 301 n.46, 394 n.85. For Herbert, see 300, 306-7, 373, 393 and 394. His brother Alessandro had sent Pietro a copy of this much reprinted work from Paris in late 1766, early 1767 (see *Viaggio a Parigi e Londra*, pp. 224, 609). Verri's enormous knowledge of the contemporary literature on the grain trade is testified to in this work, and shows he also knew some work by Physiocrats such as Du Pont de Nemours and Baudeau, although direct citations are rather infrequent. On p. 311 n.70 he cites: P.S. Dupont, *De l'exportation et de l'importation des Grains*, Soissons, 1764; *De la liberté du Commerce des Grains*, Paris 1765; *Principes de la liberté du Commerce des Grains*, Paris, 1768; *Examen du livre intitulé: Principes sur la liberté du commerce des grains*, Supplement, August, Paris, 1768; *Examen de l'examen du livre intitulé: Principes sur la liberté du Commerce des Grains*, in Supplement, *Ephémérides du Citoyen*, Vol. 11, 1768; *Faits qui ont influé sur la cherté des Grains en France et en Angleterre*, 1768; *Lettre sur les émeutes populaires qui cause la cherté des blés et sur les precautions du moment*, 1768; *Lettre d'un Gentilhomme des États du Languedoc à un Magistrat du Parlement de Rouen sur le Commerce des blés, des farines et du pain*, 1768; *Résultat de la liberté et de*

time he wrote the *Reflections*, Verri was acquainted with nearly every important economic work that had appeared in a language accessible to him.

In many respects this substantial acquaintance with the literature was typical of the period.[29] For Verri, it was undoubtedly aided by the visit Beccaria and Alessandro Verri made to Paris and London (for the latter only), the books they sent back to Italy and the friendships they made, particularly through Morellet. In addition, Pietro Verri himself made direct contact in Italy with Forbonnais, with Condillac (for long a resident at Parma) while correspondence was entered into with Condorcet and others.[30] One surprise in this wealth of literature is absence of much direct reference to major works by the more important Physiocrats: Quesnay, Mercier de la Rivière, le Trosne, Baudeau and Mirabeau, the latter's *Théorie de l'impôt* (1760) being one important exception. However, as the *Reflections*[31] makes clear, there is a good deal of evidence that Verri was familiar with much Physiocratic thought and that he had a critical awareness of its

---

l'immunité du Commerce des Grains et des farines, Paris, 1768; *Avis au Peuple sur son premier besoin, ou Petits Traites économiques*, by the editor of *Ephémérides du Citoyen* (i.e., l'Abbé Baudeau), Paris, 1768; *Avis aux honnetes gens qui veulent bien faire*, Paris, 1768; *Lettre de M. de *** Conseiller au Parlement de Rouen, a M. de M*** premier President*, 1768; *Très humbles et très respecteuses supplications des États du Languedoc du Roi sur le Commerce des Grains*, 1768.

[29] See F. Venturi, *Settecento riformatore*, pp. 690-91, 740; and cf. my "Turgot, Beccaria and Smith," in *Italian Economics Past and Present*, edited Peter Groenewegen and Joseph Halevi, Sydney, Frederick May Foundation for Italian Studies, University of Sydney, 1983, pp. 48-53.

[30] See *Viaggio a Parigi e Londra*, pp. 335, 345, 346, 645, 651 which indicates that Condillac had met Verri and other "Pugni" at Milan on his return from Parma to France. Alessandro Verri wrote to Pietro in 1767 that a copy of *Il Caffè* had been presented to Condorcet while Condorcet's works contain two of his letters to Verri debating aspects of Verri's *Reflections*. See below, introduction, p. xxv-xxvi. See *Viaggio a Parigi e Londra*, p. 593, for a reference to Trudaine's meeting with Verri in Milan in 1770. Morellet corresponded with the Verri brothers and Beccaria and sent them a copy of his *Prospectus* for the never completed *Commercial Dictionary* which was issued in 1769. In view of the acquaintance between Verri and Condorcet, Trudaine and Morellet, all friends of Turgot, it seems surprising that no real contact was made between these two like-minded economists. See above, p. xiv n. 18, p. 115 and n. 73).

[31] See above, notes 27 and 28, and below, Reflections, esp. pp. 8-9 and notes 2, 3. However, it is certain that Verri would have read Quesnay's articles in the *Encyclopédie* (for reasons, see my "Turgot, Beccaria and Smith," p. 58) while Alfonso Longo, one of the "Pugni," corresponded with Mirabeau (F. Venturi, *Settecento Riformatore*, p. 674). The absence of any direct reference to the work of Mercier de la Rivière is particularly puzzling (see below, *Reflections*, pp. 60 n.30, 107 n.63).

substantial importance. The notes provided to its text below are in part designed to identify the authors to whom Verri refers indirectly in a work where direct citation is strikingly absent.

THE WRITING AND PUBLICATION OF THE *MEDITAZIONI* IN 1770-1771

The history of Verri's *Reflections* has been chronicled in detail by Venturi,[32] and only an outline is therefore presented here. On 10 October 1770 Pietro wrote to his brother Alessandro that his head was full of good ideas on economics, perhaps an embarrassment of riches because of the problems of selection it entailed. He was satisfied with the quality of the principles these ideas contained. Both ideas and principles were the results from the previous decade of thinking on economics, in particular the five years of active, applied economics while a member of the Supreme Economic Council. Verri felt the time was now ripe to condense this experience into principles pure and applied by way of a volume of reflections on political economy. Such a work he thought would gain for himself the European reputation already won by his friend and rival, Beccaria, through his *Dei delitti e delle pene* and more recently, his *Ricerche interno alla natura dello stile*. By contrast to Beccaria, little of Verri's work had by then been published and much of that was published anonymously. However, the slender *Meditazioni sulla felicità* of 1763 was to be followed by a more ambitious *Meditazioni sulla economia politica*. This would compete on Europe's intellectual stage as an instructor in the principles of that new science which Beccaria had been appointed to teach in the Palatine School of Milan during the previous year.[33]

Verri wrote his *Reflections* in less than one month, perhaps the major reason why it lacks the citations and references to sources so frequently included in his earlier works. By October 20, 1770 he was able to announce to his brother Alessandro that the writing was

---

[32] This is, "Le 'Meditazioni ... de Pietro Verri." As indicated earlier, this section draws heavily on this authoritative study.

[33] See the reference to this in the *Reflections* (below p. 107 n.64). The jealousy motive as inspiration to some of Verri's writings is discussed by Venturi, "Le 'Meditazioni'," pp. 530-31 and cf. his *Settecento riformatore*, pp. 706-7 in the context of Beccaria's fame from his 1764 book; see also p. 747. The rivalry and tension between the two friends is captured neatly in Venturi's telling description of their relationship as "amici-nemici" (e.g., p. 731).

finished. By November 7th, the recopied and corrected manuscript was on its way to Alessandro in Rome, and the two brothers discussed its contents over the remainder of that month. The Livorno publisher, Aubert, had indicated a willingness to print the book, and the manuscript was sent to him on December 5th. A printed title page and table of contents arrived in Milan on January 22, 1771 for Pietro Verri's inspection but printing proceeded only slowly and it was not till April 20th that Verri received a box with sixty completed copies. On April 10th, a printed copy had already been sent hastily to Rome to brother Alessandro, and many other early copies went to friends in Paris and Italy in the subsequent week. Recipients included Trudaine, D'Holbach, D'Alembert, Diderot, Helvétius, Marmontel, Condorcet, Thomas, Keralio and Morellet, all persons Alessandro and Beccaria had met in Paris in 1766. Copies also went to Frisi, Lomellini, Count Radicati, his former teacher Roberti, Colpani, Beccaria, and his father. Members of the government like Molinari, Firmian and Kaunitz were not forgotten. Verri likewise sent a copy to his initial source of inspiration in economics, General Henry Lloyd.[34]

Personal reactions and reviews came quickly. Alessandro commented on the difference in style which could be noted between the first and second part of the work, the second part referring to the last 11 sections of the *Meditazioni* on finance and taxation. In May 1771, the first review appeared in the Tuscan journal, *Novelle Letterarie*, and though brief, was favorable. A much more extensive review followed in another and more prestigious Tuscan journal, *Giornale de'letterati* (1771, No. 4, pp. 81-109) and this, above all, singled out its "modernity" as the major characteristic of Verri's work. In Palermo, a further review appeared inspired probably by the Lombard, Bianchi, (*Notizie de'letterati*, No. 3, January 1772). It also praised the book as being a further important contribution to political economy or that "most useful and necessary knowledge for the happiness of

---

[34] Venturi, "Le 'Meditazioni'," p. 532. Although De Felice, p. 127 reports Voltaire's reaction to Verri's book "as the truest, wisest and clearest" he had ever read on the subject, a letter to Verri by Voltaire cannot be found in Theodore Besterman (ed.), *The Complete Works of Voltaire*. Voltaire Foundation at the Taylor Institution, Oxford, 1976. Cf. however, *Viaggio a Parigi e Londra*, p. 662 where Voltaire's thanks to Pietro Verri for sending him a copy of his *Meditazioni* are recorded and precisely dated at 19 March 1772 on the authority of A. Mauri (*La dottrina economica di Pietro Verri*, Milan, 1929, p. 240 note). Verri admired Voltaire greatly and was much annoyed that Beccaria and Alessandro omitted to visit him, despite letters of introduction from D'Alembert and Morellet (see *Viaggio a Parigi e Londra*, pp. 361, 375-76, 609).

mankind." to which Hume, Cary, Melon and Genovesi had already contributed so much. Foreign acknowledgement came with a review in the *Journal encyclopédique* (Volume 6, September 1772, part 2, pp. 314-5). It reported that this anonymous work by a Milanese *savant* contained "excellent and profound discoveries on every part of political economy." Initial reaction to Verri's book could not have been better. [35]

Further Italian versions of the *Meditazioni* rapidly appeared, but some of these seem to have been arranged by Verri himself. As early as April 1771 a reprint appeared in Naples. A further reprint appeared in Milan, an exact replica of the original Livorno text apart from corrections of the first edition's many printing errors. Finally, 1771 produced an edition published at Genoa. Attacks on Verri's book were also published during 1771. In August, there appeared *Esame breve e succinto dell'opera intitolata Meditazioni sulla economia politica*, a work particularly critical of some of the taxation material. Although without real proof, Pietro Verri generally attributed this attack to the financier Greppi, his former enemy from the Tax Farm administration whose profitable investment in tax gathering he had spoiled through his role in the abolition of the Tax Farm just over a year before. More important was an edition with critical annotations which appeared in Venice. These were the work of Gianrinaldo Carli, Verri's former friend and contributor to *Il Caffè*, whom he had transformed into an enemy through his constant criticism of self seeking behavior while serving under him on the Supreme Economic Council from 1765.[36]

Carli's notes, which number more than sixty, range from a single sentence to paragraphs almost as long as the sections on which they comment. They cover virtually every part of the book, starting with the conjectural history, development of money and the definition of trade in the early sections but concentrate particularly on criticism of Verri's policy proposals for free internal trade designed to stimulate circulation of wealth through removal of domestic tolls, customs duties and other trade barriers. They also provide a factual critique of Verri's treatment of the exchanges and population and political criticism of his support for enlightened despotism which Verri saw as such an essential prerequisite to the achievement of

---

[35] See Venturi, "Le 'Meditazioni'," pp. 532, 540-51.
[36] Venturi, "Le 'Meditazioni'," pp. 551-61.

reform. Verri's reply to these critical notes appeared in the second Livorno edition published in 1772, to which were added the material on Henry Lloyd's *Essay on the Theory of Money* (1771) and the remarks by Frisi. This addendum hints at a considerable similarity between the two books—by Lloyd and Verri—published in such distant places in the same year. Examples include their mutual description of money as the universal commodity and as the vehicle for general circulation. It also notes differences between the texts such as the relationship between population growth and circulation which in Lloyd is far more precise and criticizes aspects of Verri's price theory. These matters have been extensively discussed by Venturi[37] and need no further examination here. Aspects of Frisi's notes are discussed later.

The comparison Frisi made between Lloyd's *Essay* and Verri's *Meditazioni* does require further comment to draw attention to Venturi's detailed analysis of the resemblance between aspects of Verri's work and Lloyd's unpublished manuscript essay on government. This work emphasised the nature of societal development from the savage state, the importance of money and trade for that gradual progress towards civilized society, and may explain the considerable attention which Verri paid to such development mechanisms. Aspects of these matters can be ascribed to Verri's admiration for the work of Rousseau and his acquaintance with the economics of the Physiocrats. It seems, nevertheless, very likely, as Venturi argues, that in significant parts of his economics Verri's debts to his friend's manuscript appear to be substantial. Apart from the subjects already mentioned, Verri's discussion of the importance of a reasonable degree of equality in the distribution of property is a good example, particularly since this distinguishes his work from the Physiocrats (by its implied critique of the unmixed blessings of large scale farming) and brings it closer to the work of Lloyd.[38]

Likewise the undoubted importance of Hume's writings to Verri's *Meditazioni* needs some comment in this introduction. Verri's

---

[37] Venturi, "Le 'Meditazioni'," pp. 561-67 on Carli's notes, pp. 567-80 on Verri's response through textual alterations to the first edition, pp. 582-86 on Frisi's appendix comparing Lloyd with Verri. As indicated earlier, Carli's notes are reprinted with the text of Verri's *Meditazioni* in Custodi's *Scrittori classici italiani*, Vol. XV; the Frisi appendix and extract from Lloyd are reproduced in Vol. XVII, pp. 369-83.

[38] Venturi, "Le 'Meditazioni'," pp. 532-38; below, pp. 21-4 and note 8. Cf. however, above, p. xv on his *Sulla Felicità* and n. 21.

tremendous respect for the work of the Scottish philosopher has already been noted. He himself clearly confessed this admiration when ranking Hume among the great figures of the French Enlightenment together with D'Alembert, Voltaire, Rousseau and Helvétius.[39] This admiration for Hume is, however, tempered by criticism. Some of this can be appreciated from the correspondence. For example, on November 3, 1770 Pietro wrote Alessandro that he had shown Hume to be in error on the proposition that commodity prices rise in proportion to the increase in money in a state by demonstrating that such an effect only followed sudden increases in money supply not associated with increases in domestic productive activity.[40] In addition, Verri seems to have criticized Hume on the adverse consequences of rising money supply on the growth of exports, on the benefits of public credit and public banks and especially on commodity taxation.[41] In spite of this Hume was clearly one of the more important influences on Verri's economic writings.

After the corrected edition of 1772 with its polemic against Carli, no new editions were prepared until Verri collected some of his major writings on philosophy and economics for publication under the title *Discorsi del Conte Verri ... sull'indole piacere del dolore; sul felicità, e sulla economia politica* for publication in Milan in 1781. An interval of close to a decade had clearly removed the need for the reply to Carli and required a work which could be simply judged on its own substantial merits. The greater part of the text was therefore restored to that of the first edition, though a few changes may be noted. These included minor corrections to section II on the role of money in increasing trade; the critique of the Physiocrats in section III was accentuated; the analysis of prices in section IV was tightened. However, the vigorous defence of more equality of section VI was maintained, and the only other real casualties of the new version were the elimination of Frisi's appendix with its extract from

---

[39] Letter from Pietro Verri to Alessandro Verri, April 31, 1767, in *Viaggio a Parigi e Londra*, p. 389.

[40] Venturi, "Le 'Meditazioni'," pp. 539-40 and n. 38; for Verri's demonstration, see below pp. 41-42, 52-53, 55-56. It need not be pointed out that Verri's depiction of Hume's position is rather inaccurate on this matter and that Hume in fact shared Verri's position on this subject.

[41] See below, pp. 43-4 and n. 17; 51-52 on public credit and pp. 108, 109 and notes 66, 69 and p. 112 n. 71 on commodity taxes.

Lloyd.[42] As already indicated, it is this text, in a sense an authorized version because it was the last prepared by Verri himself, which has been translated here, although, as likewise already mentioned, a variorum edition which reproduces the changes in text, Carli's notes as well as the text of Frisi's appendix and notes would be a very useful addition to the Verri literature.

SOME SPECIFIC REACTIONS TO VERRI'S *MEDITAZIONI*

Three specific reactions to Verri's work may also be mentioned. The first is the critique of Condorcet provided in two letters written to Verri in the early 1770's. The second is the debate, of some importance in the development of mathematical economics, which followed publication of Verri's *Reflections* and Frisi's notes. The third is some reference to Ferrara's comment on Verri when he reprinted Verri's *Meditazioni* in his library on economic classics in 1852. Brief examination of these matters forms a fitting conclusion to this general introduction to Verri's economic reflections.

Two letters by Condorcet on Verri's *Meditazioni* are extant. The first dated November 7, 1771, records his thanks for the first edition of the *Meditazioni* Verri had sent him. In this letter, Condorcet indicated the pleasure with which he has read Verri's work and expressed the hope that it would soon have a French translation to enable wider diffusion of the benefits from its contents. Condorcet also summarized the contents of the *Meditazioni* by listing the two principles it had so clearly established: first, identification of the ruler's interest with leaving his people every freedom consistent with the constitution; secondly, that wise laws and just administration are the best means to increase annual reproduction and hence the strength and revenue of the State. Condorcet did provide some criticism of Verri's arguments, seeking permission to do so as a "fellow geometer." This related to Verri's principles of price where Condorcet questioned the complete proportionality asserted by Verri in the direct relationship between price and the number of buyers and the indirect relationship between price and the number of sellers. In this, as in other cases, Condorcet argued, geometry fails to lead to precise conclusions and in fact, induced error. Condorcet returned to this matter when thanking Verri for sending him the

---

[42] Venturi, "Le 'Meditazioni'," pp. 592-93 and see below, p. xxvi and n. 43.

second (1772) Livorno edition, which contained the notes by Frisi. He then argued that neither the facts nor logic supported Verri's proposition that prices varied directly with the number of buyers and inversely with the number of sellers, or for that matter Frisi's attempted proof. This was because mathematics was rather difficult to apply to explaining commercial transactions though in dealing with facts quantitative analysis was very useful.[43] This criticism is especially interesting in view of Jevons' identification of Condorcet as an early minor mathematical economist.[44]

Frisi, as implied in the preceding paragraph, had attempted a rigorous demonstration of Verri's proposition of the determination of price in terms of the number of buyers and sellers. Frisi showed to his own satisfaction that

$$P = C/V$$

where P is price, C is the number of buyers and V that of sellers by adjusting this relationship to the following form,

$$P = M(C+A)^m/(V+B)^n$$

where P,C and V are defined as before and M, A, B, m, n are constants. This formula yields nonsensical economic results unless A and B are zero, hence Verri's demonstration is more or less correct. Frisi also investigated the condition for maximum or minimum prices, only deriving in fact the condition for a stationary price.

Frisi developed the mathematics of two further Verri propositions, both demonstrating the close association between the calculus and viewing economic problems as maximization/minimization problems. In section XXI of the *Meditazioni* Verri had asserted that the principal objective of political economy was "to increase annual reproduction

---

[43] Condorcet to Pietro Verri, 7 November 1771, 1773 in *Oeuvres de Condorcet*, edited by A. Condorcet-O'Connor and M.F. Arago, Paris, Didot, 1847, Volume 1, pp. 281-89, esp. 283-84, 286-88. Condorcet also criticized Verri's view on the ease of deregulation when dictated by the popular opinion of many people. See below, Verri, *Reflections*, section IV, esp. pp. 14-18 (the reference to geometer is on p. 17); section XXXVIII, pp. 113-15. It should be noted that the 1781 text here translated made the criticized relationship an approximate one, and not the precise proposition Condorcet criticized, presumably a consequence of this correspondence.

[44] See Jevons,. *Theory of Political Economy*, fourth edition, London, Macmillan, 1910, p. 323 and cf. Theocharis, *Early Developments in Mathematical Economics*, pp. 70-71.

as much as possible with the least possible labour" that is, "given the amount of reproduction, to achieve it with the minimum of labour, given the amount of labour, to achieve maximum production." Writing R for annual reproduction, T for the quantity of labour, and treating A and B as constants, this can be expressed as

$$R + AT = B \text{ or } R = B - AT$$

and when $dR=0$ and R is a maximum, $dT=0$ and T is a minimum. In the context of Verri's section XXVI on optimal distribution of population Frisi demonstrated that the functional relationship between the distance of people and the degree of industry there postulated took the form of a hyperbola, though he warned that this relationship could only apply over a part of the function since neither industry nor distance could be infinitely large. Verri's work inspired mathematicians other than Frisi, but he himself never engaged in such speculations.[45]

There is no need to summarize the contents of Verri's *Reflections* as a whole. The enjoyment of that discovery can be left to the readers themselves. There is much that remains relevant to the contemporary economist, particularly in the current era of deregulation where Verri's council of avoiding undue haste in such matters remains particularly appropriate. Similarly, his reflections on tax reform reveal the accumulated wisdom of a practical tax reformer on the necessity of taxation for civilized society, on the detrimental effects of so-called voluntary taxes like public lotteries and other forms of State organized gambling, and on the need to temper simplicity with justice and administrative requirements. In this, and on a large number of other subjects treated in his *Reflections* he is a sound member of the eighteenth century European liberal tradition. He produced perspectives similar to the economic writings of Smith and Turgot. This was clearly expressed by Ferrara who argued "Count Verri, if he is not a classical economist, is nevertheless one of those people who, by the breadth of his knowledge, by the rectitude of his mind, by his

---

[45] See Verri, below pp. 66, 75-77 and for the reference to his price theory, the reference to section IV in the previous footnote. Frisi's argument in the text is summarized from Theocharis' account in *Early Developments in Mathematical Economics*, pp. 27-34 and see pp. 34-49 for his discussion of further developments in early Italian mathematical economics inspired by the Verri-Frisi analysis of price determination.

xxviii

untiring industriousness, by the purity of his aims, is linked to Sully, Colbert and Turgot, if it is possible to make such a comparison given their differing dimensions between the Duchy of Milan and that great country and kingdom." In addition, Verri's work never ceased to surprise Ferrara, with the "moderation, orderliness and tidiness of his thoughts, the simplicity with which he expressed them, ... which assures him, according to me, the decided superiority in any comparison with the other Italian economists of his time ..." A greater tribute from the nineteenth century editor of these Italian economists' writings is hard to imagine.[46]

SOME COMMENTS ON THE TRANSLATION AND GENERAL ACKNOWLEDGEMENTS

As already indicated, the text of the translation is based on a 1964 reprint of the 1781 edition, bearing the slightly different title of *sull economia politica* or *della economia politica*. Irrespective of this change in title, there is no doubt that this text constitutes the third and final edition of his *Meditazioni sulla economia politica* which Verri prepared. The need for a more scholarly, full variorum edition, has already been mentioned.

In translating this text, Barbara McGilvray and I have tried to keep an eighteenth century flavor in the language used, but have not checked fully whether our translation conforms to both Italian and English eighteenth century usage of language. We have also tried to stick to Verri's punctuation and sentence construction whenever possible, in order to leave the English version as similar as possible to the complexity and elegance of Verri's literary style. The italics liberally used in the translation are those of the reprinted version of the Italian text.

The notes to the translation are all *by* the editor. In contrast to his other writings, Verri did not provide a single footnote to the *Meditazioni* nor did he cite any economic writer by name. The notes partly attempt to provide references to the literature based on what is known about Verri's acquaintance with the economic writings of the period. They also provide cross references to other sections of the text where Verri explicitly suggests a need for this. The page numbers in square brackets at the end of some lines indicate the

---

[46] Francesco Ferrara, preface to *Trattati italiani del secolo XVIII, Bibliotece dell' Economista*, Series J, Volume III, Turin, 1852, pp. xviii, lxiii (my translations).

page numbering of the Italian text of the 1964 Feltrinelli edition from which the translation was made.

A number of acknowledgements may conclude this already long introduction. First, I must express my gratitude as editor for the tender care with which Barbara McGilvray managed the various drafts of the translation and sought assistance in this difficult task from several colleagues in the Italian Department at Sydney University and others whom she could interest in the task. Without her efforts, there would be no English translation of Verri's text. Her assistance was made possible through a financial grant from the University of Sydney Research Fund for 1985. As partners in this edition, we both likewise express our gratitude to Professors Gianni Vaggi (University of Pavia) and Roberto Scazzieri (University of Bologna) who read the translation in full and saved us from several mistranslations. Professor Scazzieri provided me with proofs of his introduction (with Professor Quadrio-Curzio) to an edition of the early monetary works of Beccaria and Verri they are currently preparing for publication. Finally, as editor I wish to acknowledge my enormous intellectual debt to Professor Franco Venturi, whose own research on this subject provided a tremendous inspiration and who commented on some aspects of this project in correspondence. His carefully researched study of the editions, reactions to and discussions of Verri's text which he gave me in offprint in 1981 when in Canberra, and his splendid account of the amazing adventure of General Henry Lloyd made me realize more fully the importance of the omission in not having an English text of this important classic of economic literature. After reading the text of Verri's *Meditazioni* in English made possible through the assistance from those mentioned, most readers will agree with the assessment of Verri from Francesco Ferrara already quoted. They will likewise endorse the remarks on the Verri monument which describes him as "philosopher and historian who sought after and wrote the truth to the benefit of all; honest and zealous magistrate whose informed effort and magnanimous counsel allowed both nation and state to flourish."[47]

---

[47] The inscription of the Verri monument is cited by Ferrara, *Trattati*, p. xix, n.2.

REFLECTIONS
ON
POLITICAL ECONOMY

VERRI'S PREFACE TO THE FIRST LIVORNO EDITION, 1771

Perhaps this book may lead to another better book: it would require time, which I do not have, to improve upon the organization of these ideas, which seem to me to be true, and not unworthy of public curiosity. I shall well have deserved public attention if my thoughts should serve to bring about more frequent discussions of these important subjects. Happy is the society where discussions of virtue are more common, and arguments regarding the prosperity of the State more familiar: the honor of being a good citizen is more precious to me than that of being a good writer, an honor to which I am not sure that my powers permit me to aspire. If, in these reflections of mine, there are some ideas which throw light on the true public interest, I beg my reader to set them against the rough, unfinished elements he will find here, and forgive me for these. Would that I could say something useful! Would that I could do something useful!*

VERRI'S PREFACE TO THE SIXTH LIVORNO EDITION, 1772

In extending communication to the new continent, Columbus changed the politics of Europe; and, unjustly perhaps, the question of whether, in so doing, he did more good than harm to the people of Europe has been looked upon as a problem. The discovery of fabulously rich mines, the endless profusion of precious metals that flow from there each year, the increase in money, the creation of new wants and new hopes: all these new factors having shaken up industry and given men's activity an impetus it had never before known—have promoted greed. Everyone knows what changes have

---

*All the works on public economy are accessible to everyone, unlike those concerned with ideas and knowledge that are remote from the general way of life of the people, and separate from the relationship between society and human kind. The principles of this science have an influence on the happiness or unhappiness of men, and the consequences arising from them, whether good or evil, may be greeted with gratitude or with complaint by those who will feel their effect. As stated in the preface to this work, the aim is to stimulate a better one, and in following up this noble idea it has happened that those maxims which seemed far removed from the generous instinct of those who wrote them, have been corrected. Such is the manner of thinking of men who care only for the truth, and delude themselves that this is the only way they can earn recognition, even from those who may think differently.

occurred in both minds and customs since that time. New relationships have emerged between States; the wealth of kingdoms is calculated to better know their level of security and prosperity; trade has come to be considered a public objective, and finance part of the law; reason is occupied with illuminating these matters, whose importance and influence on the happiness of human kind is generally known, and a body of knowledge called *Political Economy* is created.

At the beginning of the work, we have isolated facts and information relating to different States. Then come the universal theories to which the human mind rises once a long series of facts are well known; next, there emerge those who link theories harmoniously together, and gradually by imperceptible degrees, lead our attention firmly from ordinary notions to those more remote and most important: this is the story of every science, and the genesis of every truth.

Political economy, it seems to me, is close to becoming a science; all that is lacking is the method and organization of theorems to give it form, and it would not be so difficult today to fill the gaps and turn them into a succession of even, comfortable steps. I wish my powers were equal to the importance of the argument and the sincere desire I have to be of use; but unfortunately I feel that they fail. Nevertheless, these ideas of mine may provide the opportunity for thought, and the material for building: the warm acceptance they have already received from the public has made me decide to revise them in this edition, in order to clarify and refine a number of areas which in the first draft appeared rough and incomplete.

Anyone wishing to write on this subject, with the aim of throwing some light upon it and contributing to the progress of knowledge which has so great an influence on the happiness of man, will always find in me a good citizen, never a jealous writer. The objections that will be levelled at my ideas, as long as they emanate from an enlightened mind which, being master of itself, seeks to develop the truth, I shall receive with respect; and shall reject them with reasoned argument or adopt them in all simplicity. But time is much too precious a gift to be used in the creation of some miserable work which, because of its small value and the less than noble principles which inspired it, is destined to remain obscure.

PIETRO VERRI

REFLECTIONS ON POLITICAL ECONOMY

I. TRADING IN NATIONS WHERE MONEY IS UNKNOWN

Human societies which know no other needs than the physical have, of necessity, little or no reciprocal trade. A person raised in such a society, content to have secured his life from the dangers of animals, hunger, thirst and the elements, cannot even suspect that somewhere, far from his native soil, other things may be growing which could be useful in that life. And so, the nations we know as savage do not trade with each other, unless some famine or other disaster forces them to turn to their neighbors, from whom (whether by means of some complicated exchange, or out of mere humanity, or by direct force) they take away the necessaries in which they are lacking. Man does not act unless a need exists, and no need arises unless an idea exists; and ideas, among isolated and savage peoples, are limited indeed.

The more educated nations become—that is to say the greater the growth of ideas and needs among the people—the more trade we see introduced between one nation and another. Need, or in other words the sensation of pain, is the goad used by Nature to arouse man from the indolent state of stagnation in which he would otherwise languish. There is little consolation in this paradox, that pleasure must always be preceded by pain, and that every nation must necessarily be wretched before it becomes civilized. For us Europeans, this inevitable tribute has already been abundantly paid by our ancestors, and we can rejoice in the progress we are making in civilization, we can enjoy its benefits and increase them as much as is possible—for such will always be the task of the enlightened lawgiver. The excess of wants over the ability to satisfy them is the measure of man's unhappiness; and no less so, of the wretchedness of a State. Primitive people are [130] seldom unhappy, because their needs are few; but nations which have acquired numerous wants in the course of becoming civilized, must necessarily seek a greater power to supply [themselves] in order to draw closer to happiness. It is not my purpose here to show what means a lawgiver may usefully employ to make the desires of the people unite towards a single end, which is what constitutes the most effective effort of a people towards happiness. I shall speak only of the means by which a well-managed economic policy will augment the strength of any State.

Need sometimes leads men to plunder, sometimes to trade. For trade to exist there must be both *want* and *plenty*: want of the goods sought, and abundance of suitable goods offered in exchange. in savage nations, because needs are limited, so is plenty—in other words, surplus is minimal; for the primitive nation obtains the necessities of life from its own lands (either from pastoral, hunting, or agricultural activities), and its diligence will not extend beyond its annual consumption.

Once a nation begins to move away from the savage state, recognizing new wants and new comforts, it will be forced to increase its industry proportionately and multiply the annual output of its products; so that over and above its consumption, it will have a surplus which will correspond to the amount of foreign commodities it must seek from its neighbors. In this way, a country's annual production from the soil, and its national industry, tend naturally to increase along with increasing wants.

But how are these societies, just beginning to be aware of artificial wants, to achieve a balance between the values of goods received and goods given in exchange? Value is a term which indicates *men's appraisal of a given item*; but since in a society that is still unrefined each person will have his own individual opinions and wants, the notion of value will be highly unsettled, for it only becomes general if established where the [131] intercourse between societies is constantly maintained. This fluctuating standard of value must have been the first naturally occurring obstacle to the expansion of trade.

How can a neighboring society be expected to give us some of its products if it does not happen to have a reciprocal want of our surplus? Will it give up a part of its produce to receive our excess, at the risk of seeing it perish and spoil before there is occasion to use it? This is the second natural obstacle which must have prevented the expansion of intercourse between nations when they first emerged from the savage state.

II. OF MONEY AND HOW IT INCREASES TRADE

In order, then, to establish a stable and reciprocal trade relationship between one human being and another, and even more between one State and another, it was first necessary to find a way of achieving a universal notion of value, and also to find a commodity that was indestructible, divisible, universally acceptable, easy to store and to carry—in short, suitable to give in exchange for every other kind of commodity. Thus, before the invention of money, it was not physically possible to bring about a reciprocal and enduring intercourse between individuals and peoples. Among the many definitions of money I have had occasion to read,[1] I have never found one that seemed to me to correspond precisely to its nature. Some recognize money as the *representation of the value of things*: but money itself is a thing, it is a metal, the value of which is represented equally by that which is given in exchange for it; and this property of representing value is common to all the other goods that are generally exchanged. Others acknowledge money as a token and means of obtaining commodities: but here again, commodities are a token and means of obtaining money, and every commodity is a *token and* [132] *means of obtaining other commodities*. There are some who define money as *the common measure of things* but they forget that money has a value and is itself a raw material for many manufactured articles; anything that has value likewise measures, and is measured by, every other thing of value.

---

[1] Such definitions would have included the following: Davanzati: "Money, therefore, is Gold, Silver or Copper, coin'd by publick authority, and by the Consent of Nations made the Price and Measure of Things to contract them the more easily" (*A Discourse Upon Coins, ... being publickly spoken at the Academy* [of Florence] *Anno 1598,* translated from the Italian by John Toland, London, 1696, p. 12); John Locke: "Silver, ... the money of the world, and the measure of commerce" (*Further Considerations Concerning Raising the Value of Money*, 1695, London, John Murray reprint, 1870, pp. 321-22); Montesquieu: "La monnaie est un signe, qui représente la valeur de toutes les marchandises" (*L'Esprit des Lois*, 1748, Book XXII chapter 2, in *Oeuvres de Montesquieu*, Paris, du Seuil, 1964, p. 676); David Hume: "Money is ... only the instrument which men have agreed upon to facilitate the exchange of one commodity for another. It is none of the wheels of trade: it is the oil which renders the motion of the wheels more smooth and easy" ('Of Money' in *Essays Moral, Political and Literary*, edited T.H. Green and T.H. Grose, London, Longman, Green and Company, 1875, Volume 1, p. 309); A. Genovesi: "È un pezzo di metallo, di determinato peso e finezza, d'un dato nome, che ha un dato valore numerario, con pubblico imprunto, per servire d'istrumento a misurare il valore di tutte le cose e di tutte le fatiche, le quali sono in commercio" (*Lezioni di economia civile, Parte Seconda*, 1767 in *Scrittori Classici Italiani di Economia Politica*, edited P. Custodi, Milan, Destefanis, 1803, Vol. VIII, p. 316). For a detailed history of monetary theory in this period see A.E. Monroe, *Monetary Theory Before Adam Smith*, reissued New York, Kelley, 1966.

A bushel of grain is worth four *scudi*, and four *scudi* are worth a bushel of grain. Just as every length can be measured with any given length, so can value be measured by any thing that has value. It is true that we use money to measure the value of things in the way that we use the arm, the foot or the rod to measure length: but possessing an arm does not mean I have the means to acquire the length I measure; whereas if I have money, I do have the means to acquire the quantity I measure.

These definitions, then, do not apply exclusively to money, or do not cover all its attributes. A common error has been the desire to view money as something more than mere metal. Money has a stamp but receives no value from it.

Money is the universal commodity, that is to say it is the commodity which, because of its universal acceptance, its slight volume assuring ease of carriage, its easy divisibility and non-perishable nature, is received everywhere in the world in exchange for any particular commodity. It seems to me that by looking at money from this viewpoint, we define it in terms of an exclusive and peculiar property which conveys a precise indication of all its functions. I believe this is the logical definition by *genus and distinguishing characteristic* scholastically required: the generic feature is commodity, the distinguishing characteristic, *universal*.

Contracts of sale and purchase are then reduced to the simple and easily understood state of barter. The theory of money becomes very *simple*, since for a commodity to be universal, it must perforce be accepted at [133] the same value both within a nation and outside it; hence any arbitrary assessment beyond the value of the metal is wrong; hence the expense of coining comes from the same source as other public charges imposed by rulers; and hence, finally, the preference which silver deserves over copper, and gold over silver, because a coin which represents equal value with less bulk is more universal, and easier to safeguard and to carry.

Once the idea of money is introduced to a people, the concept of value becomes more uniform, because every individual measures it with the universal commodity. Carriage from one country to another becomes much simpler; for the nation from which a particular commodity is received will not refuse an equivalent amount of the universal commodity in return, and so, instead of there being two difficult and inconvenient shipments of goods, one becomes exceedingly simple. The plenty of one country is all that is required to satisfy the needs of another, even if the country of abundance does not at that moment have a reciprocal need. With the introduction of the universal commodity, societies come closer together, get to know each other, and communicate reciprocally. From this it will clearly be seen that mankind is far more indebted to the invention of money than might have been inferred from agricultural activity and that artificial organization of wants and industry, which has separated civilized societies from the rudeness and isolation of savages. All man's most worthwhile inventions, and those which have most stretched the ingenuity and power of our minds, are those which bring men closer to one another, facilitate the communication of ideas, wants and feelings, and make of humanity a single mass. Such are the perfecting of the art of navigation, postal services, the press, and before all these, money.

As transporting becomes easier, so communication grows, ideas multiply, wants increase, trade expands, and a parallel agricultural growth occurs in rural nations—the effect being always in proportion to the cause; man [134] cultivates as much as his wants require, and the greater the wants he must satisfy from the products of his land, the more he cultivates. Thus it can be seen how erroneous is the belief of some, that increased trade is harmful to agricultural progress; on the contrary, agriculture receives new life in a country where wants and industry are experiencing a period of growth.

III. OF THE GROWTH AND DECLINE OF THE WEALTH OF A STATE

In the main, two things are to be noted: *annual reproduction* and *annual consumption*. In every State, reproduction takes place through agriculture and manufacture, and in every State there is consumption. When the total value of reproduction equals the value of annual consumption, the nation continues in its original state, provided the circumstances do not change. A nation whose annual consumption exceeds its annual reproduction will decline. A nation whose annual reproduction exceeds its consumption will progress.

Some worthy writers,[2] saddened by the serious harm some peoples

---

[2] A reference to the Physiocrats, or the "Economists" as they were then called, with whose writings Verri must by then have been quite familiar. As noted in the introduction (above pp. xvi, xx, Verri did not directly cite any authors in his *Reflections*, unlike his practice in earlier and subsequent economic works. The critical comments on Physiocracy were perhaps partly directed at his friend, Beccaria, whose lectures on economics (posthumously published as *Elementi di economia pubblica*)

have suffered through excises, have gone so far as to pronounce taxes unjust and badly allocated unless they are distributed on the basis of land ownership, and by creating an abstract language, have set up the sect of economists, in which any man who does not use the plough is a sterile being, and manufacturers are referred to as a *sterile class*. While respecting much of what they have written as both true and useful, I am unable to share their view either on [135] taxation, which I shall deal with later, or on this class which they presume to be sterile. Reproduction applies as much to manufacture as it does to work in the fields. Our perception of everything in this world, whether produced by the hand of man or by the universal laws of physics, is not of actual *creation* but only of *transformation* of matter. The only elements human ingenuity finds in analyzing the idea of reproduction are *bringing together* and *separating*, and thus if, in the fields, soil, air and water are transformed into grain, this is *reproduction of value* and wealth, just as it is if the hand of man transforms the silken filament from the mouth of an insect into velvet, or a few pieces of metal into a reproducing machine. Whole cities, entire states, survive solely on what is produced by this highly fruitful *sterile class*, a production which includes the value of the raw material, consumption proportionate to the labour involved, and also that portion which serves to enrich those responsible for manufactures and those who employ their skills and talents therein.

Let us develop these notions further. Every country's consumption each year includes not only the food of its inhabitants, but also their clothing, their furniture, and everything used in the service of the people. The total value of all these things consumed I call *annual consumption*. Likewise each year, each country reproduces through agriculture, pastoral activity and the work of artisans, whatever is needed for food, clothing, furniture etc.; the total value of these things which are renewed each year, I shall call *annual reproduction*. The argument relied upon by the writers mentioned above who refer to the manufacturing class as *sterile*, is that the value of any article, according to them, is a quantity equal to the raw material plus the food consumed by the artisans during manufacture. On this supposition, the wealth of the State after including the manufactured article remains exactly the same as it was previously, when the component

---

had a strong Physiocratic flavor. For Verri's other critical remarks on the Physiocrats, see below, pp. 9-10, 87, 96 (and n. 56), pp. 108-9 (and n. 65) but cf. p. 113 (and n. 70).

parts were separate.[3] I believe the error of this [136] reasoning lies in the fact, or rather the assumption, that the manufacturer sells his work at no more than the bare price which will reimburse him for his expenses and consumption. Let us observe the peasant who works the soil with his hands; he is descended from twenty generations of peasants as poor as himself. It would be a rare thing if he were to end his days in greater luxury than he began them; from this it can be seen that the peasant is compensated for his work solely with his consumption, and no more. But an artisan with even a minimum of skill and good sense changes his destiny, and if he is unable to enjoy a better fate, he plans it for his children. We will not find a succession of many generations of manufacturers remaining at the same level of wealth; which shows that the price the artisan receives secures him not only compensation for what he has consumed, but an extra portion as well, and this portion is a new value quantity created within the volume of annual reproduction. In fact, if the artisan were only to receive reimbursement for his consumption as the price of his product, he would not earn any more in a day for one kind of work than for another; which is not the case, for indeed any artisan can vary his profits by changing his work. The manufacturing class, then, cannot be called sterile. And thus the reproduction of value is the portion of the price of a commodity or manufactured article which is above and beyond the prime cost of the material and what is consumed during the making of it. In agriculture we deduct the seed and the peasant's consumption; in manufacture we deduct the raw material and the artisan's consumption; and an annual value of reproduction is created, equal to the quantity that remains. It should be noted, that although I use the term *creation*, it is not intended to be understood here in its strict sense, but with a more general meaning, because if we wished to express ideas precisely, we could not apply the term creation to what we do in [137] cultivation, both this and the work of human

---

[3] See for example, Quesnay, *Dialogue on the Work of Artisans* (1767), p. 207: "We have to distinguish an adding together of items of wealth which are combined with one another, from a production of wealth. That is, we have to distinguish an increase brought about by combining raw materials with expenditure on the consumption of things which were in existence prior to this kind of increase, from a generation or creation of wealth, which constitutes a renewal and real increase of wealth." (Meek translation, *The Economics of Physiocracy*, p. 207). Marx in his *Theory of Surplus Value*, Part 1, p. 67, commented favorably on this passage and described Verri as the first major critic of the Physiocrats (*Theory of Surplus Value*, p. 59).

hands being nothing but different modifications of matter, achieved by bringing together or separating its elements.

I have said that a country whose annual reproduction is equal to its annual consumption is in a stationary state and I added, when circumstances do not change, because if circumstances do change the nation may in any case stagnate; and this would occur if a neighboring country were to become wealthier and more powerful than it; for strength and power, like all other qualities whether of men or of States, are simply relative, comparisons between one thing and another. Similarly, such change could occur if there were a decline in population, where the decrease in numbers of producers was accompanied by a proportionate diminution of consumers, so that an equal quantity would be subtracted from the value of each side.

When annual consumption exceeds annual reproduction, the country must of necessity decline, since every year its capital will be diminished by consumption over and above the yield. But it is obvious that this situation cannot last beyond a certain limit, nor can any country continue indefinitely to carry a loss in respect of another country, for either consumers will be forced to leave in numbers corresponding to the national debt, or else they will be forced to become producers, in order to redress the situation. In this case, the problem provides its own incentive for the remedy, and if the nation fails to take action the population must be reduced, and the State weakened, until the balance is restored. If consumers leave, the nation will achieve a balance as the population diminishes and moves towards its own destruction; if, on the other hand, there is an increase in producers, the balance will be reached as the State grows in strength and prosperity. Just as with the machine that is the human body, when a powerful rush of blood threatens to burst veins and arteries, it is possible to avert disaster by reducing the volume of fluid or increasing the elasticity of the vessel wall, so in the body politic, when [138] we consume more than we produce, order may be achieved by either lowering consumption or increasing production.

Man lives, albeit in a weakened condition, when healing has been effected by bleeding; so does the State. The very disorder caused by consuming more than is produced is an incentive to produce more, because the more sales are assured, the greater the incentive to the producer's industry, and the assurance of sales increases along with the number of consumers. In this case, as I have said, the nation receives a spur towards good from the ailment itself, and when legislative or economic obstacles destroy this natural path towards the public good, there must be a reduction in population and a weakening of the State until the balance is restored.

Furthermore, in a nation where annual reproduction is greater than consumption, the amount of universal commodity must increase; and as it becomes more common and familiar there than in adjacent countries, the prices of products will gradually rise until other countries cease to buy, and look elsewhere for their supplies. This is what would occur if the universal commodity were to lie around idle, which will be discussed later.[4] But universal commodity acquired through industry increases wants, because each person's wants increase as his desires multiply, and desires multiply along with the increasing probability that they will be satisfied, and this in turn increases as the means of satisfying desires multiply; hence, any person who acquires more money will increase his consumption; and so reproduction will also increase proportionately, because sales are seen to increase; therefore, particular commodities will multiply proportionately as the increase in the universal commodity becomes widespread, and the number of contracts of sale and purchase will increase as there are more means to implement them, as we shall see;[5] thus it would seem, that universal commodity acquired through industry will compensate for and rectify deleterious effects more swiftly if it is divided amongst a large number of people, than as a single large amount. In this way Nature, if left to itself, would be a benevolent mother to all men, correcting excesses and [139] defects wherever they occurred, distributing good and ill according to the wisdom and activity of the peoples, and leaving only sufficient inequality between them to keep desires and industry moving; as in an ocean, where the action of the heavenly bodies varying their horizons causes the waters to cross alternately, so that submergence is prevented. But the political obstacles which result from that fatal (even if respectable) love of what is excellent and perfect, which sometimes causes lawgivers to stray, can always intervene to a greater or lesser degree (but in all cases sufficiently) to delay and obstruct that equilibrium towards which all things, the moral as well as the physical, tend.

---

[4] Below, section XIII, p. 42.

[5] Below, section XIII which is completely devoted to the influence of monetary circulation on production, and cf. pp. 46-7.

IV. FIRST PRINCIPLES OF TRADE AND ANALYSIS OF PRICE

Just as every contract consists of a transfer of property, so trade, in the physical sense, implies the transportation of goods from one place to another. Such transportation is effected in proportion to the profit to be obtained from it. This profit is measured by the difference in the price of the goods, for no country will ever carry its commodities to a neighboring country unless it is paid more than the local price; for the cost of carriage, the responsibility of organizing it, the delay in receiving payment, and the risks inherent in the delay will not be borne without recompense. Once the components of the price of things are fully known, the driving principle of trade will be known, and we will have grasped the trunk of this great tree, to whose branches perhaps too much attention has been devoted.

Price, strictly speaking, means the quantity of one thing which is given in order to obtain another. If in a country where money is unknown, a bushel of grain is exchanged for three sheep in summer, and in autumn four sheep are demanded for the same bushel of grain, then I say that in that country the grain is purchased at a *higher price* in autumn, while the sheep are purchased at a *higher price* in summer. Before the invention of money, there could be [140] no notion of either *buyer* or *seller*, but only of the proposer and supporter of an exchange. After the introduction of money, the name *buyer* was given to the person seeking to exchange an amount of universal commodity for another commodity, and the person seeking to exchange any other thing for universal commodity was called the *seller*.

In contemporary society, which uses the universal commodity, the meaning of the word *price* is *the amount of universal commodity given for another commodity*. This is the case because people generally do not realize that the price of the universal commodity is itself variable, and the complaints that are heard among peoples everywhere are only concerned with the generally high price of all goods. What people do not see is that such protests, universal as they are, prove in fact that the price of the universal commodity has fallen.

The *ordinary price* is that which allows the buyer to become seller and the seller to become buyer without noticeable loss or gain. For example, if the ordinary price of silk is one gold florin a pound, I put it to you that a person possessing a hundred pounds of silk is as wealthy as one having a hundred florins, since the former may quite easily obtain a hundred florins in return for his silk, and likewise the latter, by giving his hundred florins, can obtain a hundred pounds of silk; were one of the two to have more difficulty than the other in making the exchange, then I would say the ordinary price was no longer one florin per pound. The ordinary price is that by which neither of the contracting parties is made poorer.

It is worth reflecting that the ordinary price since it depends on the views of many people, can only be arrived at in the case of commodities which are generally traded. Other scarce and less frequently used commodities have, of necessity, a more arbitrary and unsettled price, being dependent on the views of only a few people, without the equalizing influence of the comparisons provided by a free market wherein vast numbers of reciprocal interests are brought into conflict.

What then are the factors which determine price? Certainly it is not simply a matter of *usefulness*. To become convinced of this, we have [141] only to remind ourselves that water, air and sunlight have no price, and yet nothing is more *useful*, indeed essential to us, than these. All things which can be commonly appropriated do not have a price; therefore the *usefulness* of any thing is insufficient, by itself, to give that thing a price.

Nor does *scarcity* alone suffice to give a commodity a price. A medallion, an antique broach, a natural curiosity and suchlike objects, although they may be extremely rare and of great value to a few interested people or collectors, would nevertheless generally have a low price, or none at all, in the marketplace.

Abundance of a commodity has a bearing on its price; by the term abundance [or plenty], however, I do not mean the absolute quantity of it in existence, but rather the *amount offered for sale*. Every quantity of goods withheld from trading has no influence on the price, and is as if non-existent. *Potential offers will only produce a potential abundance.* Therefore I say that absolute plenty is not a determinant, but apparent plenty is. More precisely, the price increases with the scarcity of the thing sought (all other things being equal).

The price of things is determined by two mutual causes, *want* and *scarcity*. The stronger these two causes are when taken together, the higher the price of things rises; and conversely, the more a commodity increases in abundance or the need for it declines, the more its price goes down and the cheaper it becomes.

It should be borne in mind that, in speaking of the market, in other words the exchange of one thing for another, we do not use the term want as synonymous with *desire*: we simply mean the *preference we give to the commodity we seek relative to the commodity we wish to give up*. Thus by *want* is intended the *excess of our esteem for the goods we desire in comparison with what we wish to give up*. Let me explain. What idea do we get of this word want if we examine it as a component of price? I have money and I desire to acquire a commodity: if I have little desire to keep the money I possess, I say [142] 1 have great want of the commodity I wish to acquire; conversely, if I have as much desire to possess that commodity as to keep the money, I suggest that the two desires cancel each other out; and the *want* bearing on the price will be *nil*, because in reality I am not making an offer. A miser has a thousand desires for a thousand luxury items, but his desire to keep his money predominates, and he will never offer a price for those items. The only influence on the price, then, is the *excess of esteem for the desired commodity in comparison with the commodity to be given up*, and its quantitative expression is called *want*. From this it follows, that in a nation where the universal commodity has greatly increased, if there is no proportionate increase in need for particular commodities, the universal commodity will come to have less value in the common estimation, and it will be necessary to give more of it for each particular commodity. Suppose there are two isolated countries without any external communications; and that each has the same number of inhabitants in identical situations, with the same climate, laws, government and customs. In one of these countries the total sum of the universal commodity in circulation is twice that in the other. I suggest that in the country with double the amount of money in circulation the prices of saleable goods will also be double. For prices to equalize in these two States, it would be necessary for wants and consumption to double in the country which has double the universal commodity, because if purchases increase in any State, sellers and producers tend to multiply proportionately, as I shall now illustrate; so that demand and offers in our two imaginary countries would then be in equal proportion. In fact, the effect of the universal commodity if it enters a State gradually through industry and is widely distributed, is to continually increase the desire for particular commodities. And so it happens that the less the universal commodity is allowed to accumulate and the more it is shared among many, the more will its value be preserved and the less will the prices of particular commodities rise. Indeed, as I already mentioned in section

III,[6] as more money accumulates generally in any country, each citizen extends his [143] sphere of wants; he begins to think of new conveniences as the possibility of providing them increases. The more a person owns of the universal commodity, the more purchases he will want to make, naturally; therefore for each purchase the universal commodity must be divided up, so that it will suffice for all purchases. This is how it happens that so long as the total quantity of money increases gradually and is shared among many people, the price of things does not increase, or at least not proportionately, nor does the value of money decrease, because as the incentive to use more particular commodities grows in proportion to the increase in the universal commodity, so will the supplies of each particular commodity multiply at the same rate.

I have said that *if purchases increase in any State, sellers and producers tend to multiply in the same proportion*; because the more buyers there are, the greater is the benefit of being a seller, and the more sellers there are, the more producers multiply. But this theory does not work in reverse; and anyone saying that *when the number of sellers in a State increases, there must also be an increase in buyers in that State* is expressing ideas which have not been fully considered. An increase in buyers enhances the interest in becoming a seller, but an increase in sellers does not bring a parallel interest in becoming a buyer. A commodity is cultivated and traded because it is wanted. But a commodity is not more sought after because more people are offering it for sale and producing it. In a country where there is an upsurge in cultivating the mind, and an expansion in the taste for reading, booksellers multiply; but for the numbers of book buyers in an uncivilized country to increase, expansion of the number of booksellers is not sufficient. What I mean to convey by the terms *buyer*, *seller* and *producer* will be more apparent in section V, where it is shown[7] that the classes are not, and cannot be, divided up so that people do not belong to different classes at different times of the same day.

Apparent plenty, that is, the plenty which contributes to the [144] formation of price, increases with the number of offers and decreases as offers decline, and consequently the number of offers can be measured by the number of sellers. To recognize the truth of this,

---

[6] See above, pp. 11-12.
[7] Below, esp. pp. 19-20.

consider that if a city had sufficient food to feed its people for one year, but this food were under the control of a single person, that single seller would bring to the market, on any one day, only a quantity sufficient for that day's sales; thus the quantity offered would be reduced to a minimum level, the *apparent plenty* would be the minimum possible, and consequently the *price* would be the maximum possible since it would depend solely on the discretion of that one despotic seller.

Now, suppose these provisions to be divided between two sellers. If they were to come to an agreement, we would be in the same position as before; but if not, then the beginnings of competition between them would emerge, because even though there might be a quite substantial profit in selling the food to half the city, it is human nature to want more. Hence, speculation develops between the two sellers to estimate what advantage there is in lowering the price, and whether the benefit from the portion [of the market] taken from the competitor outweighs the general fall in price. If a third, fourth, fifth, sixth seller, and so on, should appear in the market offering the same specific commodity, the portion each can sell becomes smaller and smaller, and likewise the loss from reducing the price, being easily recoverable through extended sales, diminishes. And so with the emergence of competition to obtain the universal commodity more quickly, the number of offers is further multiplied, *apparent* plenty increases, and the price falls.

When the number of sellers is increased in this manner, naturally enough the more there are, the more difficult it is for them to agree among themselves, and the more the increased sales make up for the decrease in price, with the result that rivalry and competition become livelier; so it [145] follows that *apparent* plenty will increase and the price of the commodity will fall proportionately. Consequently, I say that *apparent plenty is measured by the number of sellers.*

It has been said that want is measured by the excess of esteem accorded a desired commodity by those who seek it, relative to the commodity they wish to sell. This is true, but if we look at society as a whole, what rule shall we use to make a quantitative measurement of want? I suggest that, *the number of buyers* constitutes a measure which, while it may lack the absolute precision required by a geometer, is the only one which suffices for practical use as a *measure of want.* To comprehend it better, let us look at a similar example. Let us say that there is one person with an exclusive monopoly of a given commodity. We have seen that in this case the *apparent plenty* will be minimal, but if there is only one buyer, then the want too will be minimal, consequently *price* will depend upon an equal clash between two single opinions. However, if the monopolist has two buyers instead of one, he can raise his asking price, and then, as the number of buyers increases so does the *want* component of *price* (all other things being equal). Thus it is from the number of *buyers* that the quantity of *want* influencing price must be deduced.

If the number of *sellers* increases (other things being equal), *plenty* will increase and the *price* will fall; if the number of buyers increases (again, other things being equal), so will the *want* grow and the *price* increase. Thus the *price* is deduced from the *number of sellers* in comparison to the *number of buyers*. The more the former increases or the latter diminishes, the further the price will come down; and the more the former decreases and the latter multiplies, the higher the price will rise. A mathematician would put it in this manner: if the number of sellers remains unchanged, prices will be proportionate to the number of buyers; if the number of buyers remains unchanged, prices will increase in proportion to the decrease in sellers: [146] combining the two hypotheses and supposing that the numbers of both buyers and sellers are changing, the number of sellers will then be in direct proportion to the number of buyers and in inverse proportion to the price; the number of buyers will be in compound ratio to the number of sellers and the price; *the price of things will be in direct proportion to the number of buyers and in inverse proportion to the number of sellers.*

But these proportions are approximate, because strictly speaking, to satisfy mathematical precision all the buyers should purchase equal quantities. The quantities displayed by each seller and sought by each buyer are not always the same, nor does a buyer seeking a single unit have the same capacity to alter price as a buyer seeking ten units [of the commodity in question]. Even so, ten simultaneous buyers will increase the price more than a single buyer who presents himself to purchase the total amount of goods sought by the ten; and this for the reasons already given. Thus, these proportions are approximately true, and in practice they will always be found consistent with fact.

Therefore, if trade from one nation to another implies transportation of the goods; if the motivation for this transportation is gain; if this is determined solely by the difference in price; and if this price consists of a comparison between the number of buyers and the number of sellers: then it follows that a nation will find an outlet for its surplus commodities in other countries according as the number of sellers of these commodities at home is greater, and the number of sellers in the country to which they are to be sent is smaller, and reciprocally, in proportion to fewer domestic buyers and more foreign buyers. Thus, a country will receive proportionately less commodities from abroad if there are more sellers and fewer buyers at home, and fewer sellers and more buyers in foreign countries.

Linking together this chain of consequences seems to me to be a simple matter. No one would carry the goods constantly from one place [147] to another if the price where they were to be sold was not high enough to compensate for the cost of transportation, customs duties, the risk of deterioration, the interest on the capital, and in addition a profit for the merchant. The difference between domestic and foreign prices therefore provides the incentive to traffic, and the greater the price difference, that is to say the higher the price of our commodities abroad, the more we will be able to export them. Hence, in order to obtain an outlet for our surplus, and to increase our share of beneficial trade, the prices of the commodities we sell abroad should be as high as possible in other countries and as low as possible at home. Prices are low at home when we have many sellers and few buyers of the commodity domestically; prices are high in another country when there are few sellers and many buyers. On the same principle, the unfavorable national balance will decline as we consume less goods from abroad, and this will occur when the price of these goods is no higher at home, or is only a little higher, than in the country which sends them to us; and it will also happen when we have many sellers and few buyers of the commodity in question in our own State, while the country selling it to us has few sellers and many buyers. All these are no more than applications of the same principle. I am aware that this manner of inquiry is by its nature rather dry, but I hope that once these ideas are reduced to their bare essentials, and revealed in all their simplicity, the reader will not regret the trouble I have put him to. Where these elements are known, it is a simple matter to put them together in different combinations, and use them as a rule in a great many cases, where otherwise the mind would remain hazy and uncertain.

V. GENERAL PRINCIPLES OF ECONOMICS

These first principles, which seem to me to be proven, serve as the basis for many activities necessary in attempting to promote industry in a [148] people and to increase population, resources, strength and reproduction in a State. The greatest possible increase in sellers of each commodity, and the greatest possible reduction in buyers: these are the cornerstones on which all the operations of political economy turn; and although it may not always be possible to discern precisely these two ideas in proposals for, and management of, public works, the fact is nevertheless, that the thrust of all such operations is towards one or other of these two principles.

Increased annual reproduction must be the aim of political economy; and it can only be achieved if there is a quick and easy market for everything that is over and above the domestic wants of the State. This only occurs if the domestic price is lower than the price abroad. In order to achieve it, *the ratio of sellers to buyers* of the commodities in question must be as *high as possible*. At times, the workings of political economy tend to reduce the number of buyers; at other times, they increase the number of sellers. Both these means appear to lead to the same end; but I shall show later the different effects achieved by these two means, and also how every equilibrium reached by *addition* augments the life of the State, whereas on the other hand, equilibrium achieved by *subtraction* leads the State towards eventual destruction.

When I say it is best for the ratio of sellers to buyers to be as high as possible, I do not distinguish these classes in such a way that the same person may not be active in both. Naturally, every nation is composed of *sellers* and *buyers*. Every *seller* of a commodity is, and must be, a *buyer* of the commodities he consumes; indeed, it follows that every man is a *seller*, because he must be a *buyer*; for if there is no want, man does not stir from his lethargy, and he will not apply himself to work or to trading, except to achieve means of obtaining what he needs for his own consumption. Thus, a nation composed exclusively of sellers is but a figment of the imagination; it would be an effect without a cause.

Although I say that no one is a *seller* except he also is a *buyer*, nonetheless, it does not follow that in a nation which has trade with other nations, if sellers multiply, so must buyers; or if buyers multiply, so [149] must sellers. I am concerned here with the general principles of economics in promoting the industry of a people and the cultivation of a State; and so even though, vaguely speaking, every purchase presupposes a sale, and every sale a purchase, this does not mean that every domestic seller presupposes a domestic buyer; in fact, one or other may be in another country, and thus the total number of internal buyers may be higher than the total number of internal sellers, or it may be lower. A branch of trade that was purely external, that is to say where the sellers were within the State and the buyers outside it, would contribute greatly to that State's annual reproduction. It would be an excellent thing, because it would coax a new quantity of the universal commodity from the importing nation each year, to be shared among the sellers and reproducers in the selling nation; because domestic circulation would increase with the necessary consumption involved in producing the commodities; and, finally, because more citizens in the State would be maintained by the foreigner, the more people were required to produce and trade the goods in question. Reproduction consumed within the State *prevents* losses; consumption of what is not reproduced locally causes *loss*; reproduction which is not consumed, but is sent elsewhere, leads to *gain*.

I said earlier that all the operations of political economy stand upon one of these two principles: an *increase in sellers* or a *decrease in buyers*. By what means shall we try to raise the seller-to-buyer ratio to the highest possible level? Restriction and coercive laws, perhaps? Indirect legislation? These are matters worthy of our study.

VI. OF THE DETRIMENTAL DISTRIBUTION OF WEALTH [150]

The number of sellers will always be greater in a nation according as wealth is more evenly distributed there among a greater number of people. Indeed, it will be seen that in countries where disproportionate wealth stands out in piteous contrast to the stark hunger of the masses—where the people in the streets gaze up at the arrogant splendor of a select few who surround themselves with conveniences and wealth—in such countries, I say, it will be seen that sellers of all commodities, domestic or foreign, are very few; buyers, on the other hand, are many, and prices are so high that there can be very little exportation. Annual reproduction is strictly limited to the bare necessities; the soil trodden by the humble and their oppressors displays an infertile and unproductive visage; everything languishes and sleeps, awaiting either a law giver with the necessary will, ability and knowledge (a happy combination indeed!), or alternatively, those extremes of misery which, although the most cruel of masters, are perhaps the only ones persuasive enough to teach man, finally, what is the path of truth.

When a nation's wealth is concentrated in the hands of a few, it is from those few that the people must receive their nourishment, and with their arbitrary price these sellers will force the common people into poverty and dependence. A few magnates, whose wealth permits them to devour every kind of commodity, will frequently occasion monopolies and artificial shortages in that nation. No abundance and no civil liberty will be found there; trade will be unknown, and agriculture neglected. For if the disproportion of wealth arises from the distribution of landed property, I say that, in general, agriculture will never be able to prosper in that nation; for if the major landowner has the whole of his land cultivated for himself, there is a considerable danger that, instead of taking the trouble to keep anxious watch over every part of his vast property, he will leave its direction in the care of a hired manager while he himself basks secure in the lap of luxury, and everything will stagnate. And if this large [151] landowner entrusts his property to a tenant, that tenant will see to it that he takes from the soil as much as he possibly can for the duration of his lease, not caring whether the land becomes barren and a future waste. A middling owner mindful of his own needs, who is able to watch over a limited area of land, and is careful in both conservation and cultivation of his soil, may draw the maximum reproduction from it, and in this case the products originally divided among a number of owners may be supplied to the market by a larger number of sellers, and therefore at a more moderate price. Indeed, any major undertaking by a wealthy landowner, aimed at preserving or enriching an area, could be carried out equally well by a number of owners working together. Therefore, where property in land is accumulated in large parcels, agriculture will certainly be neglected; and so is the reverse true, that in any country where the land is distributed among a great many owners, agriculture will be active and industrious, even though the terrain may be difficult and not particularly fertile.

Agrarian law under the Romans, the Jubilee year of the Israelites, and various laws of Lycurgus and other ancient lawgivers, were aimed at preventing anyone from accumulating large areas of land, and at preserving the subdivision of landed property.[8] These were direct laws, useful for the purpose of preserving the republic from the tyranny of a single owner, but they are disastrous for industry. Careful adherence to permanent uniformity would remove competition and ensure that since no one had the incentive of want, everything would stagnate, and society would be pushed towards the isolated and savage state; consumption would be concentrated exclusively on domestic production, and so annual reproduction would not exceed the minimum limit represented by internal needs. Direct laws can banish criminal acts, but never vitalize industry.

When there is too much inequality in the distribution of wealth, just as in the opposite case of perfect equality, annual reproduction is restricted to the bare necessities and industry is destroyed, for the people [152] lapse into indolence, either because they have no hope of a better life, or because they do not fear a worse one.

A country which is at the center of these two extremes—in other words, where the common people are neither consigned to a life of squalid poverty nor devoid of hope of enlarging and improving their fortunes—is in a condition to respond to those fortunate impulses which spur it on to progress, and any nation which is not in this condition would do well to move as quickly as possible towards it.

The means employed to break up and subdivide estates which are too large, thus spreading the benefits of landed wealth among a greater number of people, can never be direct means; for this would constitute an offence against property which is the basis of justice in any civilized society. It can be done indirectly in the following ways: when the lawgiver treats all issue equally in the matter of order of

---

[8] It is difficult to identify precisely the various agrarian laws to which Verri here refers. The Roman law he mentions is probably the Gracchan land law proposed by Tiberius Gracchus around 133 B.C., intended to create smaller allotments out of the large area of public land the Roman republic had acquired after the second Punic war. See, for example, M. Cary, *History of Rome*, London, Macmillan, 1957, pp. 282-83. The Jubilee year of the Israelites, providing for the return of landed property to its former owners every fifty years and therefore a barrier against excessive accumulation of landed property, is a well known piece of Mosaic law given, for example, in Leviticus 25, verses 10-15. Verri's view on Lycurgus as a law giver in this context, which would now probably be disputed, was more than likely derived from Montesquieu's remark that "Quelques legislateurs anciens, comme Lycurge et Romulus, partagèrent également les terres." See *L'Esprit des Lois* (1748), Book V Chapter 5, in *Oeuvres completes de Montesquieu*, p. 545. As noted in the introduction (above, pp. xxiii and n. 28) Verri's friend Henry Lloyd also emphasised the importance of a more equal distribution of landed property and the potential inefficiencies from very large scale farming.

succession to an inheritance, without regard to sex or order of birth; when no portion of land and no asset can be immutably removed from contractual transactions; when a few privative special rights which have been appropriated by magnates for themselves, are either taken from them (if a provision exists regarding unlawful appropriation) or made the common property of a greater number of people; when a few specific directives which exist purely for effect, and mainly on foreign goods, are present more as the result of personal example of the lawgiver than of his orders. In short, when these indirect means intervene, slow though they may be at first, as long as they continue in force they will not fail to achieve the desired effect, spreading among the many those assets originally accumulated by the few.

These operations, however, are to be selected and combined in greater or lesser degree according to a people's civil constitution, for as anyone can see, while potential equality is more suited to a popular and despotic State, a monarchic and aristocratic society is better advised to retain its classes and the distinctions between them.

VII. OF MERCHANTS' AND CRAFTSMEN'S GUILDS [153]

Thus, in a nation where wealth is distributed in a salutary manner, so that the people generally obtain the necessaries of life and each person can hope, with a little industry, to enjoy some conveniences as well—in such a nation, I say, as long as the law does not encounter obstacles, the number of sellers of any commodity will be the maximum that is possible in the condition of that State. For where industry is unhampered, and able to pursue all the activities natural to it, there will be as many people participating in any profession as its profit will support.

However, in every society, in varying degrees, lawgivers have been seduced by mistaken advice in matters of order and symmetry, and have tried to mould and meticulously plan that spontaneous movement which laws in fact can never prescribe in advance, although after careful study of the political phenomena they may recognize it. This has occurred with languages, which grammarians have never been able to organize as they wished; they can only study languages which have been formed in the first place by a mass of humanity exercising freedom of choice, and subsequently analyzed by philosophers making analogous comparisons.

The notion of gathering each art and each trade into a single guild, and giving this guild its own statutes, prescribing apprenticeship conditions and the standard required for induction, at one time prevailed in every country, and indeed still survives in most. It is a notion with the appearance of wisdom and prudent caution. In this way, good services to the public, perfection in the professions, and trustworthiness in contracting would seem to be assured, while dishonest and inexperienced persons would be prevented from cheating the citizenry and discrediting local products abroad.

Yet anyone who turns his attention to a close examination of these [154] institutions will find that, in the normal course of events, their effect is to render industry among the people difficult, to allow the arts and the various branches of trade to be concentrated in the hands of a few, to subject artisans and tradesmen to the burden of a variety of imposts and to keep every form of manufacture at a mediocre level and sometimes even lower. Incessant lawsuits between one guild and another, and between a guild and its members; unnecessary and futile spending out of the common purse with responsibility for it falling back on every individual; time wasted in useless conventions and capricious offices; embezzlements from time to time by petty officials of those absurd ruling bodies; rivalries, hatred, wars against anyone who dares to be more expert or more industrious: this is the scene generally revealed by close scrutiny of the guilds. They are animated by a spirit of monopoly and conspiracy, which leads them to restrict the profits of their trading to the smallest possible group, and so just by looking at their effects, we can see the futility of the hopes that were held for them at their establishment.

Their examination of candidates, in most cases, consists purely of a fee, so that a skilled but poor citizen is forced either to leave his country, or to seek an alternative; nor does this examination protect the public against having incompetent workers approved in the relevant skills, as experience in every country has shown.[9] And my

---

[9] In this argument Verri shows that he was well attuned to the strong anti-guild feeling of the liberal economists of his day. See for example, Simon Cliquot de Blervache, *Considérations sur le commerce, et en particulier sur les compagnies, sociétés, et maitrisses*, Paris, 1758, a work ostensibly written with the collaboration of Gournay. For a more general critical discussion of the regulatory role of the guilds, see Eli F. Heckscher, *Mercantilism*, London: Allen and Unwin, 1955, esp. Chapter V sections 2, 7 of Part I; Part III, chapter IV section 2. Verri presents further criticism of the guilds below, sections IX, XXIV, p. 35 and p. 73.

remarks regarding skills can also be applied to trust, which, as soon as the temptation of profit becomes stronger than moral principles, meets the same fate, whether those concerned are [acting] alone or are members of a guild.

The only effect these guilds have, then, is to reduce the number of local sellers, consequently pushing the price of goods higher, reducing transactions, slowing down industry and lowering annual reproduction.

There is one art, however, which must not be left entirely free, [155] and it is that of the apothecary; otherwise there would be too much risk for the people's health. The task of limiting their numbers does not belong to political economy but to the development of prudent medical practice. Silversmiths, clothmakers and leather merchants will prosper more if given complete freedom, with the sole condition that the authentic stamp of the State be affixed only to gold and silver of proper quality and to cloth and leather which have been treated according to fixed laws and decrees.

The ancient privileges of art guilds, and the debts they often incur, are small matters easily remedied with a wise policy. If these guilds are burdened with a small tax, it will always be easy to find some other base to which it can be transferred without harm. Let any man be free to practice his business wherever he chooses. Let the lawgiver permit sellers in every category to multiply, and in a very short time he will see competition, and the desire for a better life, reawaken creative capacities and quicken the hands of his people; he will witness a refinement of all the arts, a fall in price levels, and the spread of plenty everywhere in the wake of competition, its inseparable companion. A tree which is artificially bound and forced into growth in the sterile squares we call gardens, will languish and grow badly as long as its life-giving sap is arrested by those fetters, but as soon as it is freed from them, the lifeblood will once more surge through its branches, the leaves will grow green, and the nourishing juices spread freely, and it will thrust its green growth heavenward, and repay with its fruit the wise hand that set nature free. It must happen in the same way in society, that everything gains strength and vigor and warmth when there are no obstacles in the way of our desire to improve our destiny, and it is left to rule securely everywhere.

The buyer's judgment is always the most dispassionate and balanced and inexpert or importunate sellers will always be isolated, and will be forced by lack of profit to either improve or quit their occupation.

[156] Thus, trade and craft guilds do not yield the benefit for which they were established, but tend to lower annual reproduction and bring a nation closer to the unproductive state. It is therefore a good thing to abolish them, and this will also have the salutary effect of increasing sellers. Must the lawgiver then ignore the subject of trades and crafts altogether? No. He will protect them with sound and inviolable laws. He will establish a simple, straightforward and inexpensive method by which every individual can call on police assistance in cases of breach of promise. He will so arrange the laws that the fraudulent bankrupt will be punished by way of example, while the innocent bankrupt and the creditor oppressed by delays will be given assistance. He will ensure that contracts are religiously observed. He will establish conditions under which traders' books must be authentic. He will see to it that products of the State do not display the public seal unless they are made in accordance with the relevant laws. He will protect approved local manufactures by exempting them from duties and by discouraging competing foreign goods with a judiciously applied tax. He will protect the manufacturer, the trader and the craftsman from any unnecessary worries about undue payments for the financiers of the tax farm.[10] He will promptly punish anyone who cheats in matters of weight, measure and quality. These are the aims of the lawgiver and the means he will use to protect the traders as a group.

VIII. OF THE LAWS CONSTRAINING THE EXPORTATION OF COMMODITIES

There is another obstacle which laws present to increasing the number of sellers in a country, and that is, prohibiting exportation of some of its natural products. It used to be thought that some of a country's necessities for consumption might leave the country with the natural movement of trade; in the case of food this fear was particularly prevalent and [157] so in almost every country, with proper paternal concern, laws were promulgated prohibiting the transportation abroad of the most valuable domestic produce. Transportation of raw materials for manufacture to other countries was also forbidden; the praiseworthy idea being, that this would help local manufacturing establishments to thrive, and prevent competi-

---

[10] Further critical discussion of tax farming is given below, section XXX, esp. pp. 90-1. As noted in the introduction (above pp. xiii-xiv), Verri himself assisted in abolishing the practice of tax farming in Milan.

tion.[11]

Either these restrictive laws are observed universally by every citizen, or they are not. If the law is generally observed, and all exportation is physically prevented, I say that the cultivation of the product in question must be restricted purely to domestic consumption, since every portion over and above this would be devoid of value. Indeed, every small owner and seller of this commodity, fearing such non-value, would fall victim to the astuteness of a few rich and active persons who would accumulate it, thereby limiting the number of sellers to a few; and so the internal abundance will be diminished.

However, if there are some people for whom the law can be set aside, or cheated, it is obvious that these few will buy up the restricted commodity, and may find it profitable to remove it from the State in large lots, thus causing the very shortage which the restrictions were in fact brought in to prevent. Politics is full of paradoxes, because the threads that link causes and effects are very slender, and because when things are presented collectively, mankind sees them confusedly and not as distinct elements.

The earth we inhabit reproduces annually an amount corresponding to universal consumption;, trade uses the surplus of one country to supply the wants of another, and the law of continuity ensures that, after periodic fluctuations, want and plenty achieve some kind of equilibrium. It is a tragic error to. think of human beings as throwing dice to decide who must die of hunger; let us view our fellow men objectively, and we will see them in a truer, more comforting light. As brothers in a vast family spread across the globe, with an instinct for helping each other in need, we will see that the great force of vegetation has amply provided us with the [158] necessaries of life. It is only artificial constraints that have managed to produce fears of hunger in nations: fears which, when something happens to increase them, will surely result in hunger even though

---

[11] Such staple policies were part of the medieval heritage of mercantilist trade policy as E. F. Heckscher, *Mercantilism*, Part III Chapter 11, has so clearly demonstrated. Laws to prohibit exports of raw materials as protection for domestic employment were also widely practiced in Western Europe, and were strongly advanced in some of the British literature with which Verri was familiar. For a sample discussion see Viner, *Studies in the Theory of International Trade*, pp. 51-56. A good example is Charles King's *The British Merchant*, which Verri knew in its French version by Forbonnais and from which Genovesi, *Lezioni di economia civile*, Part I chapter XX, probably derived his similar statement of such rules. See also below, section XXXIV, p. 101.

there may be sufficient provisions to satisfy it. The majority of shortages are not physical, but are produced by men's thinking, and it is this thinking that rules the world, and distributes happiness and misery among men and kingdoms with a surer hand than all other physical beings in combination can do.

I say that prohibitive laws are either unproductive or useless. As I have shown,[12] they induce unproductiveness because they reduce the number of sellers; it remains (for me) to demonstrate when they are useless. This happens when a State does not produce any surplus in the product of which the export is forbidden. So I say, that what is necessary for domestic consumption can never leave a nation in which trade is directed by Nature alone, because no seller will refuse to give up his goods to the local buyer (who will pay him without risk or delay) in order to go to the expense of sending the goods abroad, thereby risking deterioration in transit, and moreover at the same time deferring receipt of payment. The local buyer will also always have the advantage with regard to price, because the foreign buyer must pay a certain excess to cover the risk and expense of carriage, the duties imposed on exportation and the delay in payment; and this is the obstacle that will keep an amount proportionate to domestic needs within the State, and at a price which is always below what foreigners must pay for it.

Export prohibitions are thus obstacles to the free expansion of industry; furthermore, they are an easy source of corruption, as despotic laws always are, so it is in the interests of many citizens to see them either partially waived or evaded.

IX. OF THE FREEDOM OF THE GRAIN TRADE

With the reader's permission, I will dwell for a moment on one aspect of this matter, namely the freedom of trade in an area where writers in general[13] have not so far succeeded in calming many

---

[12] For example, section VII above, p. 25.

[13] Perhaps an approving reference to the many French writers who supported the freedom of the grain trade, particularly C.J. Herbert, *Essai sur la police générale des grains*, Paris 1755; Quesnay, 'Grains,' in *Encyclopédie raisonnée*, Paris, Briasson, Volume 7, pp. 812-31 (extracts translated in Meek, *The Economics of Physiocracy*, pp. 72-87). Verri himself had written on the subject in *Riflessioni sulle leggi vincolanti principalmente nel commercio de' grani* (1769). These were not published till 1797 during the French occupation of Milan and were subsequently included by Custodi in

popular fears. [159] The argument is an interesting one; and my reasons for saying so have, I believe, some weight. There are two evils to be feared from free trade in grain. The first is that it will become scarce at home. The second is that the price will rise so high as to oppress the people. Let us examine these two dangers.

For trading to take place, it must not only be *free*, it must be *useful*. The usefulness of traffic derives from the difference in price. We must never lose sight of this principle; and having proposed it, I say this: "Wherever trade in a commodity is free, as soon as an appreciable difference is evident between the price at home and the price abroad, a difference over and above the expenses of carriage and duties, there will be profit in carrying that commodity to where the price is higher; and as soon as there is this profit, the owners of the commodity will compete with each other for a share of it, and the greater the profit, the more intense will be the competition, until eventually the profit ceases to exist." This shows that, where trading is free, there can be no lasting significant differences in price; prices must naturally level out between the various neighboring areas. From this it follows, that when sudden increases and decreases are seen to occur in the price of a commodity in common use, and its price differs continually and considerably from one area to another, it must be said that this is an artificial movement which is the result of restrictions and obstacles inhibiting trade. In countries where this trade is free, the price of grain remains relatively stable. The unexpected intermittent variations in the price of grain found in States with restrictions cause some people to tremble at the mere mention of freedom, because they imagine that given this price variation, the State's supplies could rapidly become exhausted. This argument is defective, because it presupposes an effect even when the cause is removed.

If a commodity is transported according to the profit to be derived from the transportation; if such profit is proportionate to the amount by which the price abroad exceeds the price at home; and if this excess in conditions of freedom is the minimum possible, then it follows that, [160] given freedom of trade, the amount of grain exported will be the minimum possible; nor can there ever be a significant abundance of it in the State, unless all exportation is not

---

his collection of classical Italian economic texts. As indicated in the introduction (above, pp. xviii), citations in this work indicate the substantial acquaintance with the international literature Verri had on this subject.

only absolutely prohibited, but expressly prevented; in which case, the annual reproduction will fall by the same amount as there was surplus of grain over domestic consumption, as we have said, and the nation will move closer to the risk of future shortages.

Such physical protection, however, will hardly ever be achieved. Private interests conspire to evade the law, and officials in large numbers are always subject to corruption or fraud. A stable system finds it difficult to defend its borders exclusively by force. And so, in countries with restrictions, it usually happens that if the harvest exceeds domestic consumption, the price of grain goes down at harvest-time, because there are more sellers than buyers. Some holders of monopolies, having ways and means to escape the rigors of the law, profit from the general restrictions by taking over an industry in the grip of disaster. This done, the price rises because sellers have become few in number; the commodity then passes in large lots to a foreign monopolist, and thus the profit in transportation persists, because the foreign sellers have not increased in number. So the same quantity which would have stabilized prices if freely traded, is exported without prices being stabilized, and the domestic price, being lower than the true ordinary price, will extend the circle of foreign trade relations; and the restricted nation, thus obliged to supply nourishment to far-flung populations, will be in danger of shortages at home. Such is the sequence of events which is produced from direct and restraining laws.

Moreover, if people are appointed to issue export licenses for grains, so that once the needs of the State are covered, there will be an outlet for the surplus, this idea (which at first sight appears most prudent) in practice will not prove feasible. It is not possible to calculate even approximately each year how much grain will be harvested; consequently, even if the actual annual consumption is known, no one can say how much [161] surplus there will be in any year. Further, this highly imprecise calculation will only be made some months after the harvest. Thus, every grain export license will have to be suspended for the entire period preceding the calculation —in other words precisely the time the landowners will have been forced under pressure of need into selling—and before there is a chance to trade the grain, it will all have been accumulated by the monopolists. This is why countries only allowing grain exportation under license, expose themselves very often to the risk of either emptying the country of it, or cause a shortage of buyers and a decline in this most important branch of agriculture.

No matter how free its trade and traffic may be, the State is never lacking in commodities in the quantities it requires, including those most essential to the life of the community such as oil, wine, cloth, clothing etc. Why then is it feared that only the commodity *grain* will leave the State, and fall short of its requirements, if the law does not hasten to prevent its exportation? It might be said that grain is a more precious commodity than any other. Note however, that it is only as precious to us as it is to our neighbors, so that if equal quantities are added to both sides, our relationship with other countries will remain exactly the same as for all other, less precious, commodities.

The necessaries of life can never leave a nation as long as it has freedom of trade, because where there is competition there can be no monopoly. It is in the interest of every citizen to watch out for any encroachment of individual rights, and so great is the number of those vying with each other to share in the profits, that those profits are always spread among the maximum number of people; consequently, it is not possible in free countries to achieve the large scale warehousing seen in countries with restrictions. If commodities are exported from a free country, therefore, they go out gradually, in many separate lots; and as demands for them increase, the price gradually rises, for there can be no clandestine activity where every man has the incentive of profit to [162] watch out for encroachment by others. In the markets, contracts are made openly, and so the local price of goods will rise sufficiently to make it no longer worthwhile for foreigners to buy them; and, by the very nature of things, any exportation will be prohibited at the first sign of danger that more than the surplus may leave the country. Indeed, other countries will always have to pay for our commodities what we ourselves pay, plus *carriage* and *duties* on exportation, plus the *risk* and the *delay* in payment. The relations of any State with its neighbors are contained within a certain circle, and each State adjoining us becomes the center of another circle, and so on from neighbor to neighbor. This continuing chain means that once our price has risen for some reason, the neighbor will turn elsewhere for the rest of his needs.

Some people hold an opinion which may amaze, but not convince, and that is that freedom is worthwhile for infertile countries, but dangerous for fertile ones.[14] Consider the fact that countries which do not produce grain nevertheless possess it, because they receive it from other countries; and the portion necessary for their consumption which they have received from abroad, could not leave the State without risk of famine. Thus the necessary portion either cannot go out, or else, in fact, it can. If not, why praise constraints in fertile countries? For the only export they will prevent is of the surplus to the ruin of cultivation, or else, through the monopoly-holders, they will allow some of the necessary part to leave as well as the surplus, and cause a shortage which would not have occurred if this levelling process had been left to the nature of things. Further, if it is held that necessaries should be allowed to be exported. freely, where then can this freedom be abolished if not in countries where the first bushel to leave could be the death-warrant of a citizen?

It is astonishing that, in the course of weaving the whole network of constraints in past centuries, no one has ever thought to restrict the preservation of seed corn. Indeed, according to the coercive principles which do not assume a tendency towards [the public] good as inherent in the nature of things, but rather try to impose it upon them, almost anything [163] may be said, in order to strike fear into the people, and persuade them to see a constraint on grain for sowing as a most healthy and beneficial thing. The grain to be sown is a major part of the harvest, making up one-quarter of it at least. "And what will become of the State?" you may ask, "if this germ of the future harvest is removed from the granaries and squandered through carelessness and greed? Profit is always an urgent incentive, and people will sacrifice next year's wants to those of today. Therefore every possessor of grain must deposit a proportion of it in the care of the State, to be used for sowing his field." This has never been done, however; and has it resulted in a shortage of grain for sowing? Never. Because when each persons's private interest coincides with the public interest, it is the surest guarantee of public welfare.

If it is not the lack of grain that is feared, but the exorbitant prices that could result from freedom, these fears too are unfounded. In a State with restrictions, the price is low at harvest-time because, as I

---

[14] Perhaps a reference to Galiani, *Dialogues sur le commerce des bléds*, Paris, 1770 (reprinted in P. Custodi, *Scrittori classici italiani*, Vol. 6, e.g. pp. 120-22) in which such arguments are put into the mouth of the knight participating in the dialogue. Verri had noted this point earlier in his *Riflessioni sulle leggi vincolanti*, p. 280.

have said, the owner finds but few buyers for his surplus. Then when the grain is concentrated in the hands of monopolists, the local price increases because there is a daily group of buyers made up of manufacturers and most of the city-dwellers. Thus for most of the year, grain fails to remain at a price level which would be useful, or indeed necessary, to sustain the work force within the State. The effect of constraints is to raise price levels at home, while pushing them even higher in the countries which take our goods; because the effect of the constraints is to concentrate the goods in the hands of a few, each one trying to dispose of produce which is not freely disposable, and a privileged few taking advantage of the common bondage to do their own private trading, which becomes more attractive the greater and more rapid is the wealth it promises. It is futile for the law to abolish the monopolists; it may succeed in ruining a few, but they will immediately be replaced by others; the profit in such swindling is too great and there will always be too many ways for the rich to ensure that subordinate custodians of the law close their eyes. As long as there are restraints there will be monopolists, and as long as monopolies exist, the number of [164] sellers compared to buyers will remain low through the normal course of the year; hence the price must always remain high.

Let us assume what is not in fact true, and allow that the price of grain would be higher in a situation of freedom than in one with constraints. Before deciding whether it is better to have grain at a high price or a low price, we would do well to investigate which of the two is in the interest of most people in the nation, since the public interest is simply the sum of all individual interests. To decide, then, whether the public interest of a nation calls for a high price or a low one, we must observe which is greater, the number of sellers of grain or the number of buyers. Nations lacking in grain do not have laws prohibiting its trade. Therefore we are speaking of countries where grain is cultivated and there is a surplus. In such a country, I say, there will be far more sellers than buyers of grain. Every farmer will be a seller, and the number of farmers will be far greater than the number of city-dwellers; subtract from the latter all those who are wealthy, and it will be seen that supporting one poor city dweller would mean that six or eight poor farmers must suffer. That the farmers are sellers of grain and not buyers in a grain-producing country, is easily grasped. It suffices to remember that they buy neither grain nor bread, but consume bread from the grain they cultivate themselves. They pay the landowner immediately with grain, or with money obtained by selling it. To buy themselves food and clothing, they must necessarily use the money from the grain they have sold. There is so much truth in this, that in a State which has grain in plenty, the farmer will be poorer when the grain prices are lowest. With this in mind, let us ask ourselves who, over almost the length and breadth of Italy, is the most necessary citizen and the worthiest; it is the farmer, poverty-stricken, barefoot and bare-legged. What he wears is worth no more than 3 or 4 *lire*; he eats bread made from rye and millet; he never drinks wine; he very rarely eats meat. Until he takes a wife, his bed is straw; [165] his home is a wretched hovel. He lives a life of the utmost poverty, and his work is hard and tiring. He labors to the point of exhaustion until his old age, with no hope of growing richer, struggling against poverty all his days, and reaps no benefit other than that bestowed by simple living, innocence and virtue. The only inheritance he leaves his children is the habit of toil. A race of industrious and frugal men, who give the soil its value and nourish the carelessness, the whims and the idleness of city dwellers. These things, far removed from the sight of the ordinary citizen, should arouse at least as much sympathy as beggars, usually deserving of their condition, elicit from the people in the cities.

Freedom of trade in grain, then, can never in any circumstances or in any State cause harm to the country's subsistence or its abundance; nor can constraints of law ever be beneficial. Should anyone doubt the truth of these principles, let him look to experience, and he will find out that those States which have neither art nor craft guilds nor laws constraining the exportation of their products, are more thriving and wealthier, than others where such coercive organization exists, and the closer nations approach to plenty, the less such laws remain in force.

X. OF EXCLUSIVE PRIVILEGES

A further consequence arises from these principles. This is that all monopolies and all exclusive privileges are diametrically opposed to the good of a State. At first glance, it would certainly appear that a person inventing a new art might deserve the favor of seeing everyone else forbidden to compete with him and share the profits of his art. This principle of equity prevailed, and still prevails, in many States, even some of the shrewdest and wisest; but show me a crop, an industry or a skill that has [166] continued to support itself and to strive for perfection after it has been given exclusive rights. Once competition has been removed, and the creator is assured of being the only seller, there is no longer any incentive to do the job well; and just as some families, having tasted too much wealth, are ruined through carelessness, so the monopolist may easily bring failure upon himself. Either the creator of the new art has mastered it sufficiently not to fear being overtaken by anyone else, or he has not reached that point. In the first case, the privilege of exclusivity will be almost useless to him, since he already has the best of all privileges, that of excellence; and in the second case it would be an injustice to forbid all other citizens to practice the industry, in order to favor a mediocre craftsman who, moreover, might without harm be induced by the offer of a bounty to abandon his new invention, and indeed, being mediocre, might welcome this idea. And so the way is always left open for the maximum number of sellers to emerge in any area.

A further consequence of this is, that certain Powerful industries and manufactured goods which most impress foreigners and arouse their interest, are often of very little use, or even sometimes detrimental to the State. An industry which puts on a great show is a natural candidate for a monopoly, for no one will be anxious to compete with it. A hundred looms divided among ten manufacturers will be more useful than perhaps two hundred belonging to a single manufacturer, because there will be more sellers, and competition leads to improvement, and to the adjustment of price to the level most useful for the State, and earnings that are shared by a greater number of manufacturers always stimulate the activity of each one.

So I say that the number of sellers in every possible category must be allowed to multiply naturally without limits being imposed, so that the lowest possible price is reached in each category, which is the only way of increasing annual reproduction, because it ensures a market for the surplus; and this theory must, as I said, extend to every category, including sellers [167] of provisions destined purely for local daily consumption, because the price of all commodities and all foodstuffs must necessarily include the price of the farmer's or manufacturer's consumption; consequently, the abundance of each small product contributes to the overall abundance of every commodity in proportion to its popular consumption.

XI. VARIOUS SOURCES OF ERROR IN POLITICAL ECONOMY

There are two means which spring naturally to mind for achieving the best possible domestic ratio of buyers to sellers in any country, which is the original and sole objective of all the activities of political economy and the only possible source (accompanied as it is by increasing annual reproduction) of wealth and prosperity in a State. These are: *by increasing the number of sellers*, and *by reducing the number of buyers*. While it is possible to proceed openly with the former by removing obstacles and allowing activity to develop spontaneously, the latter, on the contrary, calls for extreme caution and a trial approach that allows its effects to be observed, rather than an approach using bold, masterful strokes.

In some States where it was desired to increase the proportion between sellers and buyers by reducing the number of buyers, sumptuary laws were promulgated. Experience has shown that these are at the very least dangerous and more often than not disastrous. While they do reduce the number of buyers they also cause the number of sellers to fall in even greater proportion. They may be beneficial for countries which subsist on a precarious trade balance, and for populations whose annual reproduction is so weak that they are obliged to become agents for the productive States. These they may suit, because most of the sellers obtain their profit from foreign buyers and will not lose a great deal if local consumers are removed; but in any nation where a new value is annually created corresponding to the overall [168] consumption, annual reproduction will be seen to decrease in the same proportion as domestic consumption, unless greater consumption of a local product is substituted; which the laws ought always to promote as a general custom, and although the lawgiver should not state it directly, this is the thinking which must be encouraged.

In a State where the preservative principle is *equality*, and where a citizen conspicuous for his wealth or ostentation gives rise to fears of tyranny, where widespread suspicion of encroachment prevents usurpers from emerging, I say it would be wise to sacrifice some portion of the life of the community to its security, and provident to set a limit on luxury. It will always be difficult to imagine the best government—with the utmost security existing alongside internal stability from laws and civil liberty, maximum strength and speed in repelling all external aggression, and the highest level of reproduction, industry and wealth—unless most of the effort has already been made by Nature in that locality. Thus, for the rulers of a people it is a case of choosing the lesser evils. But since I am writing of political economy, I must show how far it should go by its own efforts.

Every operation aimed directly at reducing the number of buyers, produces a temporary reduction in price, for the decrease in buyers soon brings with it a decrease in sellers, and so instead of there being increased circulation within the community, part of it remains isolated and idle, and there is a proportionate drop in annual reproduction. I shall not cite examples; the reader may find them for himself; and such is my confidence in the firmness of these principles, that I flatter myself he will not be able to find a single case in which a law directed at lowering the number of local buyers has brought constant abundance to any country.

We saw in section III[15] how countries go about adjusting their consumption to annual reproduction, and how, of the two ways this can be done, one is ill-fated and the other propitious; I say the same thing here [169] about the means of increasing the proportion between sellers and buyers. When it is achieved *by addition*, the State moves towards prosperity; and conversely, moves away from it when the attempt is made *by subtraction*. The life force of a society must not be extinguished, nor can its overall activity ever be usefully diminished. The only portion which can be extinguished with benefit is that which may hinder the development of greater activity. Provident laws limit men's activities if they obstruct the expansion and stability of overall activity. If the lawgivers were to allow fraud in contracts to go unpunished, fraudulent bankrupts to remain safe and undisturbed, and bad faith to remain in peace, the freedom allowed to these activities would have the effect of curbing a far greater number of activities; because all trading and every contract made on the assumption of good faith would be destroyed. The nature of this book does not permit me to expand on this principle, which could be extended to the entire theory of law, and could serve as a definite boundary of civil liberty: but the mere mention of it will suffice for scholars to examine its implications and recognize its extent; and therefore I say only that every reduction in the overall movement and permanent activity of a society represents a step towards its destruction.

The domestic abundance of any nation depends on an increase in

---

[15] Above, esp. pp. 11-12.

the proportion between buyers and sellers; from this follows the transport of surplus reproduction to other countries; this in turn leads to increased annual reproduction; and from this the nation derives its wealth, population, agriculture and strength. The two ways of achieving this which come to mind are: by increasing sellers, and by reducing buyers; the first method is always harmless, and its adoption is a simple matter; the second is highly dangerous and produces transitory effects, following which the nation lapses into a worse state than before. How is it, then, that men of business in the majority of countries have always tended to choose the second alternative in preference to the first? Why run headlong along the thorniest and most difficult path, when the broad, safe path is right before us? Let us look [170] into the secret depths of the human heart, and we shall find the reason: perhaps it lies hidden in such a dark recess that sometimes even those who follow it do not realize they are doing so. Restrictive and prescriptive laws represent one level of authority, and the common pride is always more flattered when it believes it is making an impression and creating activity among the people than when it is limited to merely smoothing the way and removing obstacles. To prevent some effect directly seems a quicker, more gratifying alternative, and certainly there is far more effort involved in discovering remote causes. So those who governed the cities began to act by using subtraction. With the passing of the centuries, this method became as hallowed as any ancient practice; and customs venerated by public opinion and by laws are not challenged without uncommon energy and determination; it requires a superior strength of intellect to be confident that one is not wandering alone against the tide of opposing authorities. All these difficulties were ranged against choosing the first alternative; whereas by following the second method, one was assured of never being confronted with an unfavorable result, indeed one acquired the right to all the praises normally bestowed on prudence (which in politics is generally synonymous with imitation). Natural inertia causes men to bow to the examples before them, and saves them from the effort of investigation. These reasons, singly or in combination, have ensured that in general the laws, constitutions and customs of society have concerned themselves rather with keeping a tight rein on numbers of buyers, than with removing constraints on sellers and encouraging them in unlimited numbers.

XII. WHETHER THE PRICES OF SOME COMMODITIES SHOULD BE FIXED BY LAW

It was once thought that domestic prices could be made uniform by law, in particular the prices of a few commodities most commonly used by the people. The expedient may have come into use because authorities saw that their restrictive laws were not producing general abundance, but that on the contrary, reduced numbers of sellers were resulting in rising prices. To remedy the unhealthy consequences of one restrictive law, an even more restrictive one was introduced, and the selling price of some commodities was established by those who held power. This practice still survives in some countries. Most people are seduced by the appearance of a speculative policy which, like the Sophist school of thinking, is able to dress up these instruments of restraint and present them as beneficial to the State, and so, prejudging their usefulness, with an apparently virtuous but swift decision, has them accepted.

Let us examine the effects of such regulations. Suppose the true ordinary price of a commodity is 12 *lire*, in which case, if there were freedom of trade, it would be sold generally on the market at 12 *lire*. The law ordains that the price will be 11 *lire*. Thus the whole order of things is upset; the price is no longer in direct proportion to buyers and in inverse proportion to sellers. It no longer represents the degree of esteem in which men hold that commodity. The price has become an arbitrary expression of the law, which does not do justice to sellers, and consequently tends to reduce their number. What effects will this have? Sellers will diminish; they will conform to the law as little as they possibly can; hence more than just the surplus of the commodity in question will be sent abroad; attempts will be made to adulterate the goods by mixing inferior materials with them; people will try to falsify weight and measurement; and those in charge of executing the law may, in their constant struggle against these activities, prefer to sacrifice a few victims who are guilty of some arbitrarily created crime, without however bringing an end to the confusion or establishing general plenty; for a law which is against the interests and instincts of many, can never [172] be continually and peacefully observed, nor can it achieve favorable results for the city.

Explicit price laws are unfair to the purchaser if they fix a limit which is higher than the ordinary price; they are unfair to the vendor if they set it lower; and they are useless if they keep to the true level of the ordinary price.

Many nations have experienced the evils of price regulation in the worst possible way, that is to say by suffering shortages. As recently as 1771, one province in Germany suffered a famine during which some of the people died, at a time when investigation brought to light ample grain and more than enough for their consumption; but this grain had been set aside by its owners, because a price had been imposed on it which they did not consider high enough. To me the theory appears to be clear, and as long as there is a comparison, as long as there is a *buyer* and a *seller*, it will prove correct.

Most written laws handed down to nations by their forefathers were preceded by those uncompromising words *to force* and *to prescribe*. As a result of the progress of reason in the present century, we are beginning to see some laws with the benevolent motto *to invite* and *to guide*. No matter what form of government a society lives under, it seems to me that it is in the interest of the ruling body to allow the citizenry the greatest possible freedom, and to take from them only that portion of natural independence which is necessary to preserve or improve the prevailing form of government. I believe that every portion of freedom deliberately taken from the people is an error of policy, because this wilful action of the lawgiver is seen by the people only as an act of force; gradually imitation will spread; the people's notions of morality will grow feebler, and as people lose faith in their security, they resort to cunning; wherefore, if these political errors multiply, the nation will inevitably become first of all uncertain; then it will become a sham, and finally, if power too freely exercised should reach the point of oppression, the population will dwindle and the nation will lapse into idleness. But in our present happy circumstances, following the progress made by philosophy in every area of knowledge, and with the care and humanity of today's governments, these things fortunately are not to be found except in speculation. Nonetheless, it is worthy of notice that every superfluous step the legislator takes to restrict men's actions, represents an actual diminution of activity in the body politic, leading directly to reduced annual reproduction.

XIII. OF THE VALUE OF MONEY AND ITS INFLUENCE ON INDUSTRY

We have seen how the *price of commodities* is in *direct* proportion *to buyers* and in *inverse* proportion *to sellers*. We shall presently see how to measure the *price of money*. If trade is none other than the *exchange of one thing for another*, and if an *abundance of demand*

and a *scarcity of offers* go to make up the price, *it will follow* that the *price* of the *universal commodity* will be in *inverse proportion to buyers* and in *direct proportion to sellers*; a consequence which springs directly from the principles and definitions given, since sellers are to money what buyers are to commodities, and hence the *more buyers* there are of each *particular commodity,* all other things being equal, the *lower the price money will have*; and the *more sellers* there are *of particular commodities,* again circumstances being equal, the *more highly* will *money* be valued. Thus an *abundance* of the *universal commodity* directly excludes an *abundance* of all *particular commodities,* and just as a shortage of particular commodities in any nation is to be feared, an *over abundance* of the *universal commodity* is equally to be feared.

An over abundance of the universal commodity is not measured by either the absolute quantity or the amount in circulation; but rather when the number of *buyers* has to deal with a small number of *sellers,* in other words, to the extent that sellers are in a small proportion to buyers this undesirable [174] *abundance* may be said to exist. Nature sees to it that sellers multiply according to the increase in the number of buyers; if the increase in buyers is gradual, sellers within that State will multiply naturally at the same rate. If the increase in domestic buyers is spasmodic rather than gradual, there may be a parallel increase in sellers from outside the State. Consequently, the superabundance of the universal commodity will become noticeable when it enters the country in large amounts, without allowing industry time to accumulate sellers by adding gradually to their number. Money which mounts up imperceptibly in a State is like the dew that revives and invigorates vegetation; but it is like a raging torrent, uprooting, muddying and inducing sterility if it enters the country as accumulated treasure.

From the start we have seen that lively and extensive trading could not exist if the universal commodity had not been invented,[16] and if trade had of necessity consisted in the exchange of consumable goods. Thus, a nation where money is so scarce that there is not enough for internal circulation will have to return to a savage state, and by limiting transactions purely to needs, according to the limited availability of the universal commodity, exchanges between individuals will fall off and become restricted to the lowest level, and there

---

[16] Above, section II, esp. pp. 7-8.

will be a proportionate reduction in annual reproduction; and the poor and isolated nation whose fortunes are flagging, will revert to its old ideas and go back to its beginnings, and retreat from the cultivated condition.

For the same reason, where unflagging industry and flourishing trade in a nation gradually add to the universal commodity, this will be a new spur to industry and will increase the number of contracts, encourage the flow of internal circulation and lead to the introduction of new comforts and conveniences, a refinement of the arts and crafts and the invention of ways of perfecting them and speeding up their production. Everywhere cultivation, good living and prosperity will be diffused.

We must therefore distinguish two different cases. An increase in [175] the total quantity of money will have these beneficial effects, if a nation acquires it through active industry; if it achieves the increase in a passive manner, either through abundant mineral production or by forcing other countries to pay it the universal commodity in tribute, then instead of encouraging industry it will lull its people into general lethargy. Money entering the State this way will fall into the hands of a few, and these few, overflowing with riches, will indulge in excessive luxury, scorning imperfect or crude local products and will, in expectation of general indigence, set about consuming and dissipating their wealth in foreign products and manufactures. The gift of riches will be like a flash of lightning coming down to strike the heads of the multitude, leaving the people cowering, demoralizing them; the universal commodity will pass to other countries untouched by the common people and the only tiny portion the nation retains of it, will be in the form of salaries received by a few idle citizens. The ostentation of a select few contrasted to general poverty, is the spectacle that will be offered in every place where money has been accumulated without national industry.

Considering the two quantities, *universal commodity in circulation and particular commodities offered*, it is true that the whole of one is equal in value to the whole of the other; therefore, if one of these two quantities should increase while the other remains stable, the increased quantity will be worth less. If the universal commodity in circulation increases, and the particular commodities on offer do not increase at the same rate, it will be necessary to give a larger amount of the universal commodity for each particular commodity. It appears therefore, that the price of everything must be higher according as more money is circulating in the country. A certain writer,[17] in other ways a precise thinker, once asserted that an increase of money in circulation is without exception a bad thing, and that it destroys exportation. but one fact is missing from this argument. This is, that an increase in circulating money, when it is achieved gradually and through industry and is shared generally among the people, leads to a proportionate increase in consumption; and, as we have already indicated, people buy more as they [176] are given more money to spend, and acquire more wants when they have more means to satisfy them; and the more sales a commodity finds, the more the sellers of it increase and the livelier its reproduction. Thus, if money accumulates in a State, and saleable commodities do not multiply in proportion, prices will rise; if money and saleable goods increase at the same rate, prices will remain as they were; if money increases, but saleable goods increase at a faster rate, prices will be seen to fall. Thus it follows that money which is acquired through industry animated by annual reproduction, if not prevented by political or physical obstacles, will increase and promote progress in industry to such an extent that particular commodities will multiply to the maximum and prices will fall. The more sales he makes, the more is the seller able to content himself with a small return from each sale. General rule: wherever trade flourishes, the benefits to the trader are minimal for each separate commodity, and wherever industry is sluggish, the trader's gains are lavish.

In a country made rich through industry, machines and tools are perfected to such a degree that the workman in a single day will produce an article which, in a less industrious nation, would take

---

[17] It is difficult to identify the precise author to which Verri is referring in this context; most of the famous monetary authorities whom Verri cites argued the favorable benefits of increased money supply on activity and trade. These include Cantillon, Montesquieu and above all, Hume, to whose accounts Verri must have been indebted as to a lesser extent he would have been to Forbonnais' *Elements du commerce*, Leyden and Paris, 1754 (for a discussion see Monroe, *Monetary Theory Before Adam Smith*, esp. pp. 226-35). However, Cantillon, *Essai sur la nature du commerce en général* (Higgs edition, London 1959) in Part II chapters 6-8 associates increases in money with declining exports and loss of profitable trade (for example, p.183) but it cannot be said that he generally regarded an increase of money in circulation to be a bad thing. Because Hume also stressed detrimental export effects from price rises through increased money supply Venturi ("Le 'Meditazioni'," p. 539) has suggested that Verri's remarks were particularly directed against Hume. From the fact that Carli did not append a note to this passage (see Custodi, *Scrittori classici italiani*, Volume XV, p. 126) Verri cannot have been referring to Carli in this context.

several days to make; such are the resources available to a country which has grown rich through its industry, resources that are lacking in a country whose riches have come spontaneously from the land, not by means of an increase in annual reproduction as the fruit of industry, but because fate has endowed it with the universal commodity. The former will have increased its sellers along with its growing wealth, while the latter will have increased its buyers, who, as we have seen, must have recourse to foreign sellers, those at home having unwisely neglected material riches in favor of conventional wealth.

Recognition of this truth leads us to deduce that consequently, the *value of money* does not depend on the *absolute quantity* which a country possesses, nor on the quantity circulating therein, but rather on the *proportion* that exists between *sellers* and *buyers* within that country. A further [177] consequence is that the greater the movement of circulation within a State, in other words the greater the number and quantity of saleable commodities and the more transactions taking place, the more will prices fall to the minimum possible level, if all other things are equal. The reader, whose opinion I covet and heed, does not need me to explain that the minimum possible level in a given province does not mean the lowest price in the world. Prices fall to the lowest possible level, given the conditions in a particular country, when the circulation there rises to the maximum level; but logic does not allow us to induce from this that wherever prices are lower, there will be more circulation. Prices are in direct proportion to *buyers* and inverse proportion to *sellers*, as we have said.[18] If the amount of money in *circulation decreases*, all else being equal, price will fall; if the *saleable quantity increases*, all other things being equal, again, price will fall. In short, if *buyers* decrease, or *sellers* multiply, price will go down. In a nation where prices are low, the proportion between sellers and buyers is greater than it is in a nation with higher prices; and this is the only conclusion we can legitimately draw.

It will be observed that the wealth of a nation is not so much measured by the absolute quantity of goods it possesses, as by the proportion of its goods passing between it and adjacent countries which trade with it. Thus, wealth acquired through mining will only have half the effect on the national wealth that an equal sum

---

[18] Above, section IV, esp.pp. 17-18.

obtained through trading would have, since the latter would be an amount added to that nation and subtracted from another, which implies a double amount in the proportion between the two nations.

XIV. OF THE INTEREST OF MONEY

Money then being abundant and widely distributed in a nation made rich by the activity of its industry, it will happen that many will seek either [178] to invest it or to convert it into a permanently productive estate, for the safekeeping of money is always a burden which few will happily bear, for fear of losing it; and in an industrious nation which is conscious of the full value of money and the benefits of making it bear interest, it will not be allowed to remain idle through inefficiency, as happens in more lethargic countries where there is too much inequality in the distribution of wealth. Thus agriculture will be improved, manufactures increased, offers of money multiplied and demand reduced, according as there is more money circulating in a country. And so the interest of money will be reduced; for *interest* is always *in direct proportion to those demanding money and in inverse proportion to the offers*, for the *demand* is to *money* what *buyers* are to other *commodities,* and likewise the number *of those offering money* is to money itself what *sellers* are to other commodities, and *interest* corresponds to what in the case of commodities is *price*. Thus a universal abundance of money carries with it, as a necessary consequence, a lowering of interest, and the many owners of money, no longer finding the same revenue in lending, will resort to buying landed estates, or else will use their money in manufacture. Hence the first consequence of lowering the interest of money is a rise in the price of landed property, and a new stimulus to manufacture. I say a price rise in landed property, because there will be an increase in buyers, but no increase in sellers. The stimulus given to manufacture will tend to increase the number of sellers, and thus encourage general plenty.

It would seem that the higher price paid for land ought to increase the price of the products of that land, because they are the fruit of the capital used in the purchase. But in general, the opposite will be seen to occur; in other words, as the interest of money falls, certainly the price of landed property will rise, but not the price of produce, because the increased price of properties does not lead to a decrease in sellers or an increase in [179] the number of buyers of the land in question; on the contrary, an increase in the number of the buyers of the land will result in its being distributed amongst a greater number of owners; and there we have our increase in sellers of foodstuffs. The fruit of *money* is *interest*, the fruits of the *land* are *food*; if one of these diminishes, the other must reach a balance with it; because many will compete to employ both in the most profitable manner, until they become equally profitable. Hence, estates may increase in value, and there may not be a consequent increase in the price of foods.

The second consequence of lowering the interest of money is improvement of lands, extending cultivation to areas previously neglected, and maximum annual reproduction from the soil—this is what happens if the highest interest is not to be found in loans; so we see how an abundance of the universal commodity (assuming that it circulates and is poorly rewarded if left idle in banks) can in fact produce an opposite effect to the one which seemed likely at first glance. In other words, instead of raising the prices of things, it tends to lower them and lead to general plenty and maximum annual reproduction. These are the effects it produces when it enters a nation as a consequence of general industry.

The third consequence arising from the low interest of money, is the opportunity to embark on great projects, whether in trade or in agriculture, because loans from landowners or manufacturers for bold ventures are easier to find, since the annual return corresponding to the debt incurred can be comfortably subtracted from the profit of such operations; and this leads to constant expansion, and growing markets for excess annual reproduction. Swamplands drained and transformed into lush fields, rivers contained in their courses, streams diverted in agriculture by harmless means, navigable canals excavated to facilitate transportation, daring feats of navigation, and all manner of experiments will be found in these countries, where there is plenty of money in circulation, and its interest is low.

In a State where the universal commodity is augmented through industry [180] and widespread activity, internal circulation must also increase proportionately, that is to say the number of internal transactions must multiply. In such a State, as I said earlier,[19] wants increase; the sphere of wants extends proportionately from the necessities of life to comforts and then to pleasures; the universal commodity will not diminish in value even if it has increased in

---

[19] Above, section XIII, esp. pp. 43-4.

quantity, because the wants it must satisfy have similarly increased. It is useful to repeat here, that the price of particular commodities increases when a higher proportion of *sellers* to *buyers* is achieved; the price of the universal commodity, on the other hand, increases when *buyers* reach a higher proportion to *sellers*.

We have seen above[20] that, in order to achieve general plenty and maximum annual reproduction, the first of the two possible alternatives, an *increase in sellers* and a *decrease in buyers*, must be chosen, and the second discarded; and we have seen this to be the principle used for the good and consistent regulation of particular commodities. But with the universal commodity it is necessary to do precisely the opposite; if it is to be organized in a beneficial manner, laws must come down hard on those who are to receive the money, rather than those who are giving it on loan. I do not mean by this to say that restrictive or express laws should ever be made, fixing the interest of money at a given level. This interest, as we have said, is in direct proportion to demand and in inverse proportion to offers, as price is to the number of buyers divided by the number of sellers. These are both physical effects, which can never be contradictory or disproportionate to the causes which produce them. So for the same reasons given above[21] which show why authorities cannot with impunity dictate the price of particular commodities, they cannot dictate limits on the interest of money without exposing the law to avoidance. For a law which opposes the interests of the majority of the citizens will always be avoided, and although each individual act of avoidance may have a minimal effect, when many individual elements [181] conspire towards a single end, the required effect will always be achieved. Even a cursory study will reveal this truth to us: that the stability and soundness of any civil institution in any nation, is always determined in practice by the extent of support for it, whatever the constitution governing that nation, with the single exception that in a democracy, these institutions are more silent and more covert, but this does not make them any less effective in making decisions regarding stable institutions.

---

[20] Above, section XI, esp. p. 36 where the general principle is stated succinctly.
[21] That is, above section XII, pp. 39-41.

XV. OF THE MEANS BY WHICH THE INTEREST OF MONEY MAY BE LOWERED

How then can a government lower the interest of money by working on those who are to receive it? In every country there are public debts, and there are banks from which people lending money to the State receive their annual return. Experience has shown the usefulness of lowering the interest rates of these banks, not only in order to lighten the load on the treasury, but also as an indirect method of stabilizing all the nation's loans at a lower rate.

I do not need to add here what the most obvious principles of justice will have suggested to everyone's mind, that is, that the State must have an amount available to enable it to offer all of its creditors immediately the return of their capital, should they not be satisfied with the lowered interest, which must, of course, be obtained with the creditors' spontaneous support. Heaven help the State where immediate profit prevails over the nation's true interests! Woe betide the State if public trust should weaken! Its interests will then diverge from those of each individual. A pretence will cover each citizen's indifference towards the union of which he is part; moral principles will be destroyed; the nation will fall into corruption, a condition far worse than its original savage state; everything will deteriorate; and at the first emergency, when assistance is required in the interests of [182] public safety, it will be looked for in vain. Past centuries saw examples of this in many parts of Europe, and it is thanks to the sufferings of those times that States in general now follow enlightened policies, and there is universal recognition that *public trust and confidence in the treasury are the richest and most enduring legacy of any sovereign.*

Public banks having reduced the interest of money to a lower rate, if the creditors of these banks make up a substantial part of the nation's lenders, it will come about that those seeking the universal commodity on loan will follow the example of the public banks, and no longer offer the former rate of interest; and those looking to provide the universal commodity on loan, no longer able to hope for the same interest from banks as in the past, will content themselves with a reduced rate. If the creditors of the public banks have taken back their capital rather than submit to the lower interest rates, the number of those offering to lend is effectively increased, and consequently the interest will be proportionately reduced.

There is another way in which governments can reduce the interest of money. To realize this, we have only to reflect on the two methods used to exact interest by those who offer money. The first method is to reimburse them for the profit they would have gained from investing in agriculture or trade; the second is to compensate them for the degree of risk there may be of losing their capital. We have already seen in section XII,[22] that, in a nation where industry in all its aspects is free to move, the return on trade and agriculture must be reduced to a low level. From this it follows that, according as the hope of improving their destiny is fostered and nourished in the hearts of the people, and as those things which unleash the driving force of industry are present to increase annual reproduction, the portion which the scholastics[23] call *profit foregone* will naturally diminish. Then, it is up to the lawgiver to reduce the risk known in legal terminology as consequential damage. This will be achieved through excellent laws, judicial forms that are brief and simple, and judicious choice of public officials, so that every citizen may quickly and easily assert his right; and police, always ready [183] to pounce on usurpers and those in breach of faith, can render the security of contracts permanent and sound.

Such is the truth of this, that I make bold to say that in no country where industry is lively and good faith is respected will there be a high interest of money; and conversely, wherever the interest of money is high, annual reproduction will be slow and the reliability of contracts highly dubious. From the interest of money we can estimate the relative well-being of nations.[24] The interest of money can be compared between nations and between centuries, in order to calculate the degree of well-being of a society which thinks itself cultivated; but the value of any commodity, whether universal or particular, can never be compared between nations unless there is direct communication either between these two or by both with a third nation; because *value* may be low as much because of a lack of *buyers,* an abundance of *sellers* and a *scarcity* of money as because of the *swiftness* with which transactions follow one another; nor can there be comparison between two quantities which are isolated and

---

[22] Above, esp. p. 44, cf. pp. 29-30.

[23] *Lucrum cessans* or 'profits foregone' in the scholastic literature provided a major justification for the taking of interest on money loans. See Barry Gordon, *Economic Analysis before Adam Smith*, London, 1975, esp. pp. 195-204.

[24] This paragraph was probably inspired by Hume's famous remark that "interest is the barometer of the State" ('Of Interest' in *Essays Moral, Political and Literary*, Volume 1, p. 327).

distant from each other. I say the same of anyone wishing to compare the *values* of one century with another: true, we may calculate for such a purpose how many ounces of metal were given in exchange for a certain commodity, but never the true *value* of it, if by the term value is meant the degree of esteem it had in the common view, for the esteem in which precious metals are held has varied with the passing of time, and they have become less precious as inexhaustible mines augment the universal commodity in Europe. For an exact calculation to be made of *value*, between two societies having no communication with each other because of physical or temporal distance, there must be a third unchangeable quantity to which they may be compared; as the unalterable extent of the number of hands and the constant weight of the ounce, conveyed and compared, will provide the means for calculating the true relationship between two heights and weights distant from each other: but this unchangeable quantity for comparing values does not exist, nor could it; because money itself, albeit a universal commodity, is worth more at some times than at others, and thus is incapable of serving as a measure. Custom established the principle that the value of money [184] depends on the sovereign imprint it carries, and that the prince was the arbitrator who decided its value; and according to such a principle, a man who must give back capital received in past centuries is only bound to return a sum in *lire* equal to what was paid at the time; the conclusion is soundly derived but from a false principle. The value of money was shown to depend on the value of the metal, the imprint being simply evidence of its weight and purity, and from this true principle the conclusion was drawn, that to repay an amount of capital received in centuries gone by, it would be necessary to pay as many ounces of silver as had originally been given; a conclusion which presupposes some substance in the value of the metal which, in reality, is not there. Finally, a more accurate calculation was attempted by comparing prices of the most common commodities consumed by the people in these two separate eras, and fixing an average sum for each epoch; then an estimate was made of the number of ounces of silver a man would need to take to market today, to buy the provisions which would have been bought at the time of the loan with the amount received; and it is this method which comes closest to being accurate.[25] In cases of restitution however, the courts rely on the first method of calculation, which has the advantages of long usage and simplicity, and perhaps has ceased to be unjust, since, the custom having been established in general use for centuries, when a loan was made, the capitalist bore the eventual decrease in value, for which the interest current at the time and the right to recover the money within ten years compensated.

XVI. OF PUBLIC BANKS

We have seen[26] the good effects banks can have on reducing the interest of money. The invention of banks, like the invention of bills of exchange, belongs to the last few centuries. With the coming of bank notes a *representation of the universal commodity* was introduced which is extremely convenient to [185] transport, and which, wherever credit is extended, must greatly increase circulation and the rapid turnover of contracts. As long as people believe themselves to be as rich with a bank note or bill of exchange, as they are if they possess the universal commodity, they will more readily accept these pieces of paper and promises of money in their trading than the money itself, because of the great ease of their storage and transport. Inventions of this nature will be useful to those States where the keeping of public confidence is entrusted to a large number of people who have an interest in maintaining it and who, because public opinion is behind them, have sufficient strength never to be in fear of anything; because the greater the number of people who have an interest in keeping public confidence, the more the interest they have in it; and the more certain is their action, the less likelihood there is, as anyone can see, that public confidence will be betrayed. But wherever some changing circumstances can alter the level of public trust in these representations of the universal com-

---

[25] Verri's discussion of the difficulties in comparing the value of money over long time periods foreshadows the index number solution which according to Viner (*Studies in the Theory of International Trade*, p. 126) was not discovered till 1798 by Wheatley. However, Galiani, *Della Moneta*, 1750 (Feltrinelli edition, Milan, 1963, pp. 187-89) appears to have had the idea of prices of groups of commodities (cf. A.E. Monroe, *Monetary Theory before* Adam Smith, p. 224) while Carli has also been credited with developing a system for measuring the purchasing power of money well before Lowe's attempt in 1822 (see Appendix on Carli, in P. Custodi, *Scrittori classici italiani*, reissued Rome, 1965, Vol. XIV, p. lix and the reference there cited).

[26] **Above, section XV, pp. 48-9.**

modity, there will be danger of overturning private fortunes and individual opinions; nor can such institutions without danger expand beyond a certain limit.

Banks have the effect of doubling the volume of the universal commodity they receive, since both the universal commodity itself and its representation remain within the State. So it would seem that they must cause the price of particular commodities to rise; but the rapid circulation they cause, by spreading gain over a greater number of transactions, may not only prevent prices from rising, it may even lower them through ever-increasing multiplication of sellers, and so with increased purchases, sales and internal consumption, a greater increase is also possible in annual reproduction.

If the public banks had high interest, they would be doing an obvious harm by inviting people to deposit their capital in the bank and abandon all industry. In such a case the danger of bad faith would produce a good effect, for agriculture and the arts would owe the fact that they were not abandoned [1861 solely to the fear of this bad faith. Sometimes, when states have descended to corruption, they actually derive benefit from the sources of that corruption, when a multiplicity of evil principles results by chance in two opposing destructive principles canceling each other out. This is in fact what would happen if dissipation of public funds were to alienate the people's trust; very high interest rates would have to be offered by those who wanted loans, which would ruin industry; but set against this there would be another public vice, the bad faith of the administration, and the end result would be a feeble effect, or no effect at all.

States which have the largest areas and most extensive trade with far-flung nations, have more advantage than disadvantage from public debts, as long as the people continue to trust them; smaller, more subordinate nations, however, feel few good effects from public banks, and the small benefit is largely outweighed by the treasury's annual loss due to the burden of interest; therefore, in the first case the aim must be to continue the national debt, and in the second to settle it by the least harmful means possible.

XVII. OF CIRCULATION

Our reflections have so far led us to the conclusion, that an increase in the universal commodity and its representation is always beneficial to the State if there is a proportionate increase in circulation; because sellers multiply according as buyers increase, which in turn results in increased annual reproduction. To have an even more accurate idea of the truth of this, let us recall that every seller, since he has to obtain a certain amount from his daily sales, will be able to restrict himself to a smaller portion of gain from each particular commodity according as he makes more sales; therefore, as circulation increases generally, even in those commodities each seller must consume, it will become possible to pay less profit to those selling them, and so it goes on: the salaries of workers, the price of [187] manufactures, and the profits from trade will continue to fall, and sellers will continue to multiply, as long as circulation increases. This is how an increase in money, which ought by its nature to increase the price of all commodities, in fact when it enters a country as a result of general activity produces the contrary effect, which is to lower prices and also to lower the value of money; and this for the reasons already stated, because desires multiply according as there are more means to satisfy them, and such is the continuing increase of the domestic circulation and the number of transactions that the universal commodity spreads and flows without its level rising—as when one river flowing into another produces pressure and impetus, which so increase the movement of the deep waters below the surface, that the water level is seen to fall at the very moment when it would seem that it should rise.

When a transaction takes place between a local citizen and a foreigner, it is called *foreign* trade; if the native person is the *seller*, it is *favorable trade*; if he is the *buyer*, it is *unfavorable trade*. When the transaction concerns two natives of the State, it is called *domestic trade*, or *circulation*. The circulation is the overall sum of domestic transactions. Once the nature of circulation is fully understood, how it increases as a result of growth in the volume of money acquired through industry, and how it contributes to lowering prices; once the characteristics of circulation are thoroughly understood as the effect of an increased volume of money acquired through industry, it will also be understood that an increase in the price of provisions in a nation is not proof that its national wealth has increased. In fact, this can occur either because a decrease in money is accompanied by a slowing down of circulation occurring at a faster rate, so that the profit to the seller is spread, or else because of a reduction in sellers; or, because industry slows down, and annual reproduction is curtailed. Indeed, at present we can observe that not only are protests to be heard all over Italy concerning the [188] excessive price of food, they are also heard in France, England, and in general throughout Europe; from which it may be seen, that if a province of Europe experiences this excessive price, this cannot be taken as an indication that it is ahead of other provinces in those forms of wealth considered as the constituents of a nation's prosperity and strength. Price can increase due to an abundance of money generally accumulated in Europe, without a parallel increase in abundance of particular commodities; and this increase in price does not show that any part of Europe is effectively richer, for its wealth depends on comparison with the other states.

All commodities sold in a day are equal in value to all the money that has been spent in that day to purchase them; but money is not consumed, whereas the commodities are bought to be consumed. This consideration alone is sufficient to demonstrate two truths: first, that *money never ceases to represent a consumption* except when it is melted down to be made into some manufacture -indeed, as long as it is money it represents new consumption daily without undergoing any change; second, that all the money circulating in a State is undeniably equal to the daily consumption, but it is not equal either to the annual consumption or to the annual reproduction; for the same money passing through the hands of many citizens in the space of a year represents its own value as many times as there are transactions transferring it from one hand to another. Therefore, the greater the speed and frequency with which money passes from hand to hand, the greater the proportion by which exchangeable commodities must be said to exceed the amount of universal commodity in circulation; and because wherever the universal commodity is in short supply, men are necessarily more frugal, prudent and generally cautious, foregoing many comforts and pleasures so as not to be without it, in order for rapid circulation to be achieved an abundance of money is required: which, I repeat once again, shows that when the quantity of money in a country increases as a result of industry, annual reproduction of particular commodities must always increase in greater proportion, unless some extrinsic physical or moral force intervenes.

In order to be convinced of this truth, that is, that the amount [189] of money in circulation in the State is much less than the overall value at which goods for annual consumption are sold, we need only look at the number of people who on the first day of the year have sufficient cash to cover their expenses for the ensuing twelve months. Very few, certainly; perhaps scarcely one in every thousand inhabitants, and that one would be a bad manager of money. How many are there on the first day of the year who possess barely enough money for their provisions for a single week? All those who till the soil, all wage-earners, all small craftsmen, almost all the common people in both city and country. Thus it is only through movement and circulation that sufficient money can be supplied to settle the transaction for any year. When the volume of money shared among the many is increased, wants, needs and transactions, as we have said, will also increase; and the annual reproduction and the amount of particular commodities will continue to multiply at an ever-increasing rate, according as the circulation of the universal commodity gains momentum. If the amount of *annual reproduction* and the quantity of *universal commodity* in circulation are known, the rapidity of the movement of circulation will also be known; indeed, if any two of these elements are known, the third will be known also.

So we may ask ourselves, whether the use of gold and silver objects and money collected in caskets and removed from circulation, constitute a good thing or a bad thing for the State. My answer is, that under a prudent government these things must always be bad, since for the urgent needs of the State, one citizen may not be obliged to contribute more than another, unless it is on the basis of a valuation of the apparent taxable assets of everyone in general; and then the entire profit which might have been hoped for from these treasures disappears. Whereas, if they were circulating in the State, they would provide a spur to annual reproduction, and spread the true and real foundation of national wealth and power over a wide area. As for gold and silver objects, it will be better in this case to provide examples than to introduce dangerous sumptuary and restrictive laws; and the effect of example cannot be doubted; for no nobleman will spend money on these luxuries as long as the magnates are leading a simple life, and this they will surely do, to the extent that the lawgiver in his practice prefers the [190] luxury of comfort to that of ostentation.

I hope I shall be forgiven for returning so often to first principles. The more generally money is distributed among the people, the more their wants and needs increase, because man desires comforts according as there is a likelihood of securing them. The more the people's needs increase, the more they purchase and the more they consume: the more they purchase and consume, the more profit there is in being a seller and the more sellers multiply, and the more sellers multiply, the more the annual reproduction also tends to increase. An *increase in money* alone and in isolation tends to cause prices to rise. *Circulation* contributes to lowering prices according as it is more rapid. These two quantities, according to their combination, can either increase or reduce the price of things or keep it constant.

XVIII. OF COINED METALS

Thus it is wise, though never with direct laws, but rather indirectly, to ensure that money stagnates as little as possible, and that it is kept in rapid movement in order to increase the number of transactions. By the term money, or rather universal commodity, however, everyone will understand that I refer only to the noble metals, gold and silver, because money made from copper, or from silver diluted with a large amount of alloy, cannot merit the name of *universal commodity*. It will be a native *commodity,* peculiar to one country, and will never be sent out of that country because of the expense of transporting it. Therefore, if a country were to conduct its trading with copper money, it would approach conditions prevailing before the invention of the universal commodity; there would be very few transactions, restricted almost to the bare necessities, and they would be exchanges more often of one thing for another than of articles for money, because of the inconvenience of keeping it and the weight and volume involved in transporting it. Annual reproduction would be strictly limited, circulation extremely slow, the population small, and industry unknown. Conquering armies might emerge [191] from among those men who cared little for life because its pleasures were almost unknown to them. No nation could thrive as long as it remained in that condition; it must either revert to the savage state, isolating itself and abandoning the notion of wants as they are known in civilized nations, or else carefully remove all obstructions and allow that ferment of hope and need to rise up in the people out of which comes the industry that breathes life into a society.

According to this principle, gold coins will increase circulation more than silver, and bank notes, provided they are generally accepted, will increase it even more than gold. Among metals, then, gold coinage is more desirable for the State than silver, and silver than copper, always preferring small volume and greater value.

From the beginning of the Christian era up to the sixteenth century I do not believe silver was ever considered for coins intended for large payments: the museums, at least, do not show us anything other than small silver coins, rarely exceeding the weight of two *paoli*,[27] which appear to have been used as fractions of gold coins and for payments of small amounts not covered by gold coins. The only silver coins we do occasionally see are large silver medallions, for the most part post-dating the discovery of America. The use of large silver coins was introduced during the time of the Emperor Charles V, and increased subsequently.

In many European nations it is customary to have some part of the coinage in copper, to be used for smaller transactions among the ordinary people. If monetary law establishes the value of coins correctly, in the self-same value proportions as each piece, indepe dently of the stamp upon it, would have in Public transactions, there would be no need to fear either transfer of the money outside the State or the introduction of foreign money, because no trader will ever take on the expense of transportation unless out of necessity, or for profit. If it were for necessity, to settle a debt, a law prohibiting it would lead to breach of faith which would discredit the country; if for [192] profit, this could only represent an increase of money in the State at the expense of a less prudent nation which had put an arbitrary tax on the metals.

To clarify these principles still further, we must remember that, as we have said many times, in every State the annual *consumption* and the annual *reproduction* must be taken into consideration. If the surplus of our annual reproduction is not equal in value to the commodities and products we receive from elsewhere, it will perforce be necessary for some of the universal commodity to leave the State in order to balance our accounts with respect to the other States, and to forbid the export of money would be tantamount to removing the effect while leaving the cause.

Moreover, in a State where an ounce of pure silver always has the same value as another ounce of pure silver, whatever the stamp and denomination of the component units, and whatever their volume may be as a result of mixing the silver with inferior materials; where the same can be said of silver, gold and copper coins; where the

---

[27] A paolo was a silver coin used in Florence and Lucca, 1½ of which were equivalent to a Florentine lira. See Carli, *Dell' origine e del commercio delle monete*, in P. Custodi, *Scrittori classici italiani*, Vol. XIII, Table I (facing p. 190). It seems likely that Verri's statement about the prevalence of large silver coins derived from this source. The accuracy of Verri's general observations is supported in Alexander Del Mar, *The Science of Money*, reissued New York, Burt Franklin, 1968, pp. 62-79.

proportion between one metal and another is commensurate with the nominal price of the metals; where, in short, the lawgiver has confined himself to indirectly *stating* the public price of the metals, never directly *regulating* it; in that nation, I say, not a single ounce of gold or silver will ever go out except to make way for an equal value of either universal or particular commodities, or indeed for a greater value if a higher than fair value has been placed arbitrarily on the coinage sent out, and a lower than fair value placed arbitrarily by the foreign countries on the coins received from them: for it is no more feasible for the lawgiver to fix the price of the universal commodity arbitrarily than to fix that of any particular commodity, since as we have already seen,[28] this quantity depends on the number of buyers compared to the number of sellers. Wherever coining laws become merely a statement of the nominal price of the metals, there can be no confusion with regard to coinage, nor will trade in coin ever be harmful. Nevertheless, the definition of the nominal price should be remembered. The variable nature of the price of the universal commodity [193] means that a fixed price list of coins can never be a good law for any length of time, because as circumstances change it becomes a false statement, even though it may originally have been true.

It is of no consequence to the convenience and wealth of a nation whether coinage carries one stamp or another; in fact, small nations pay too high a price for their vanity in having their coat of arms on minted metals, for the expense and loss involved in the minting either fall on the public purse or else are reflected in a proportionate reduction in the intrinsic value of the metal minted; which reduction will never be taken into account by other countries, and consequently such nations will see their currency rejected by other countries in trading, unless they give it at a lower price. Thus it is my belief that in small States, coins should not be used for any operation, other than an exact calculation of prices, and that any coins should be accepted in transcriptions as long as they are valued as *pure metal*. In large kingdoms however, it is indispensable to have a mint in operation, and to support its cost, in order to keep the greatest possible amount of metal in circulation and in that way multiply transactions to the maximum; as a result of which, it is worth repeating, sellers increase in number; and from this comes internal

---

[28] Above, sections IV and V, esp. pp.15-18.

abundance, which facilitates exportation, which alone can push annual reproduction to its upper limit: and this is the only true and stable basis of the wealth and strength of a State.

In fact a large kingdom will either have mines, or it will have an extensive trade leading to the introduction of precious metals that have not been coined; and so there is raw material for the mint; and the need to redress the wear and tear of the coins from use means that the workshop will not remain idle and will, as I said, add to the amount of money in circulation. But a small State, which has no mines, must either melt the metals it has purchased or melt down foreign coins in order to strike its own; in the [194] former case, an equal amount of money goes out; in the latter, an equal amount of money disappears; if the same money compensates for the expenses of minting, it will accordingly have so much fictitious value, which will count for nothing, among foreigners; if compensation is sought by a proportionate reduction in worn coins used as ready money and in small transactions, this will be rejected by foreign countries, and in the case of a small State will bring an increase in the number of noble coins. So I say that small States, provided that in establishing price they have set the value of each coin in circulation at the ordinary price of the metal, are assured of having the best system. If the *gigliato* [a coin stamped with the Florentine lily] is worth ten *lire*, the *lira* will be one-tenth of a *gigliato*. If a *gigliato* is 70 grains of pure gold, the *lire* will be seven grains of pure gold, or one hundred and five grains of pure silver, given the proportion of one to fifteen, and everybody will understand what a *lira* is, without there being any need for a coin of that name.

The workshop in a mint is the only one nobody wants to pay to have built; yet its construction is an absolute necessity, since without it, pieces of metal tendered in payment would have to be not only weighed, but assayed, and there would be no universal commodity. If the States of Europe were to agree to put a certain value on the manufacture element in coins, then those countries rich in mines which sold unminted gold and silver as particular commodities, could supply the raw material to the workshops; but until this happens, mints will only be able to recover the cost of their work when some of their coins are valued above their intrinsic worth.

XIX. OF THE BALANCE OF TRADE

Various authors[29] have written about the balance of trade and the method of calculating whether a nation's wealth is increasing or decreasing. The excess of exportation over importation, and vice versa, is commonly called the balance of trade, an expression which, as someone has wisely observed,[30] is in truth neither precise nor accurate. Every nation's imports must [195] always equal its exports, and the value of all the goods coming in must, after a certain lapse of time, be equal to the value of all the goods going out. It is a simple matter to understand this truth if we remember that *money is a commodity* and that debts are paid. My ideas succeed one another, and anyone who does not perceive the sequence as a whole will not understand me. These imported or extracted commodities, then, include also the universal commodity; and just as we have seen that an increase in the amount of money in circulation multiplies contracts and consequently increases annual reproduction, so a decrease in that same money must bring with it a fall in annual reproduction. As a consequence of this, the nation which balances its importation of particular commodities with universal commodity will suffer loss; and conversely, if it balances the exportation of particular commodities by importing universal commodity, it will gain. By the term balance we mean *a comparison between two quantities*, that is to say between the total value of *imports* and the total value of

---

[29] For a detailed discussion of aspects of the literature in England on the balance of trade before Adam Smith, see Jacob Viner, *Studies in the Theory of International Trade*, pp. 6-15, and Bruno Suviranta, *The Theory of the Balance of Trade in England*, Helsinki, 1923. There was also a substantial French and Italian literature on the subject, of which Carli, *Brevi ragionamenti sopra i bilanci economici della nazione* (in P. Custodi, *Scrittori classici italiani*, Vol. XIV) can be particularly mentioned. Verri himself had carried out a detailed statistical analysis of the balance of trade for Milan in a paper written in 1764, *Bilancio del commercio dello Stato di Milano per il 1752* only extracts of which were reproduced in P. Custodi in his *Scrittori classici italiani*; a full text edited by L. Einaudi, did not appear till 1932.

[30] Although the context suggests that Verri means the balance of payments always balances when monetary transfers are included, he may also have been referring to Mercier de la Rivière's discussion of the balance of trade which argued that over the longer run, exports and imports must inevitably balance. See *L'Ordre Naturel Essentiel des sociétés Politiques*, pp. 576-77. Similar sentiments are expressed by David Hume, 'Of the Balance of Trade,' in *Essays Moral, Political and Literary*, Vol. 1, pp. 330-31. Carli (in Custodi, *Scrittori classici italiani*, Vol. XV, pp. 174-77) appended a long critical note to this passage.

exports, the achievement of which would always be unreliable and arbitrary if it were to move away from simple arithmetical principles. Nor can a State ever hope to reach a balance with the same accuracy or by the same method as a private family. A family's balance is achieved by comparing what it had in its possession, minus its debts, with what it now possesses, again minus the debts; but it will be obvious to anyone that it is not possible for human ingenuity to calculate all the existing particular and universal commmodities in a nation and the debts owing to foreign countries. To be absolutely precise, the balance of trade in this sense cannot be ascertained; but we use the term balance of trade in our attempt to discover one fact: whether the country is moving towards good or towards ill; and it was thought that the answer to this question could be found by carefully comparing the particular commodities brought in with those sent out, so that by converting both of these to their probable value, the difference arrived at could be taken as the amount of money which [196] must have been added to or removed from the State.

A comparison between particular commodities exported and those imported will show a State whether the value of the goods it has sold to other countries is greater or less than, or equal to, the value of the goods it has purchased from them. This information reveals whether a country is heading towards prosperity or towards decline. The State in which annual consumption is greater than annual reproduction is in the situation of having in actual fact reduced its wealth, and it may be compared to a family when, as well as its annual income, it spends part of its capital.

If all the goods imported and exported were written up accurately in the customs registers, we would be able to tell from a perusal of these the ratio between the value of annual imports and that of annual exports; but in many countries this does not happen, and various items of trade, direct products of the soil or manufactured articles, are not recorded in the registers, because they are exempt from duty. But even if every particular commodity were recorded, the universal commodity could not be included, and it may leave a country to be used in foreign banks or to purchase property, or enter it to go into local banks on behalf of other nations, or to buy property for them; and although none of this is part of either annual reproduction or annual consumption, it can have the effect of accelerating or slowing down internal circulation according to the principles previously discussed.[31] Thus, it is a factor which needs to be known if the increase or decrease in a nation's annual reproduction is to be calculated. An examination of customs records is therefore not sufficient to provide this important knowledge.

Nevertheless, even though this examination does not tell us a great deal, it is always a most useful exercise. Clear thinking is necessary for conceiving a justifiable method of proceeding with a form of calculation involving so many elements, dividing each commodity into classes and taxing each according to its likely price. Note that I said clear thinking is [197] required for a *justifiable* method of proceeding that will encompass so many elements using arithmetic, because any counting operation which lacked precision and where the amounts declared were not the final result of a series of connecting links beginning from primary elements, any procedure which assumed credibility on the basis of mere statement without proof, would obviously not provide a base to support any reasoning at all. Certainly the scrutiny would be more interesting if it showed us not only the totals of particular commodities exported and imported, but also the countries of destination and origin to which they were sent and from which they were received; but to complete this arithmetical operation in a way that would provide proof and evidence requires too much time and expense, and the potential usefulness of the result of such analysis is quite small and less reliable than it appears.[32] Not all commodities are received direct from their country of origin, and they are shown on customs registers as coming from the city they left most recently, which inevitably results in an error in the register. Nor are all the exported commodities, which have been domestically produced and grown, always sent directly to the destination finally intended for them and where they are to be consumed: and this is another source of error, because they will then be found from the registers to be debited to the account of a country where they were only in transit. The third source of error arises from inexperience of carriers and drivers, from whom little accuracy is to be expected; and all they have to go by is what is written in the customs registers. These three inevitable and vast sources of error must exist in such an estimate, and since no one has a complete list

---

[31] See above, section XIII esp. pp. 42-4.
[32] Verri's authoritative comments on these practical difficulties in computing a balance of trade arise from the fact that he himself had carried out such exercises with respect to Milan for 1752 and 1762. See the reference cited in note 29 (p. 60) above.

of the relations of any country with each of the other countries trading with it, what is the use of such listings? Precisely none, because where we believe ourselves to be creditors, a banker's draft may have made us debtors, and vice versa. If, in order to arrive at an apparent operational listing, the essential is omitted, that is to say the true computational organization which ensures the veracity of the totals by referring back to the separate elements, then a bad deal has been struck, because the *real* will have been abandoned in favor of the *apparent*. The State is an enormous family; the important thing is to know with [198] certainty at the end of each year whether things are getting better or worse, which items are losing money and which are a source of strength; the names of creditors and debtors are not important in the least, and the country of origin of commodities is more or less known. I believe, therefore, that an examination of customs registers must be effected which distinguishes every commodity together with its price, and carries a single commercial distinction between debit and credit; let me repeat, however, that the calculation should not be arbitrary, but the appropriate one in every statement. A document prepared according to these principles will inform the able politician of the true current state of a nation's industry, and this list alone can tell him which areas need immediate support, which are flourishing and increasing, and which section of the population it would be preferable to assist, either in agriculture or with manufacture, so that all areas of annual reproduction will be maintained in as prosperous a state as possible. Without such a list, no one will know which class of people to turn to, and it is possible for part of the national industry to be considerably reduced before the authorities realize it.

Without this annual list, there could be no soundly-based estimate of the effect for the treasury from reduced tax on some particular commodity, and consequently either a risk would have to be taken every time that particular tax was touched, or else no support could ever be given to the interests of annual reproduction, which in changing circumstances might require certain alterations in commodity taxation. Thus, although an examination of customs registers is something which ought to be done, it is not possible to deduce from it with accuracy whether the annual reproduction for the year concerned is increasing or decreasing; for even if particular commodities exported are of lesser value than those brought in, it may be that more of the universal commodity is brought into the country than went out of it, and the national industry would in that case receive new stimulus to augment circulation and reproduction.

XX. OF THE EXCHANGES [199]

The rate of exchange is another method used by some to discover the state of annual reproduction. To have some idea of a subject that has been rendered obscure, both by the special terminology used, and by the minute detail in which it has been treated by some writers,[33] we need only reflect that the debts which merchants have with foreign traders can be easily balanced if the same number of foreign traders have debts of equal value towards local merchants; for the local merchant hands over his debtor to his creditor, without any transfer of money between the two nations concerned. But if, once the credits and debits with other countries have been calculated, the nation still remains in debt, then the two areas of imports and exports must necessarily be equalized, and the country will have to send money outside its borders; and this transfer involves both risk and expense. In such a case, anyone wanting to have a sum of money paid to a foreigner must bear the burden of the transport costs; and should he wish to commission a trader to make this payment, he will need to pay that trader the cost of the transport involved. A person requiring a bill of exchange for a foreign country must therefore pay more than the amount which will be disbursed in the other country. In this case a loss is incurred on the exchange.

Let us suppose the opposite, that when all debts have been paid, the nation remains a creditor of foreign countries. In this case, since the transport costs of the money are the responsibility of the foreign country, what will happen is that in order to save this risk and expense which are always borne by the debtor, the foreign nation will prefer to pay on the spot a little more than it owes; and so, to obtain a bill of exchange payable by a foreign country, one spends something less than the amount that country will actually pay out; and then we say that the exchange gains.

If a nation's exchange could be in a constant state of either gain

---

[33] Examples with which Verri was likely to have been familiar include Cantillon, *Essai sur la nature du commerce en général*, Part III, chapters 2, 3; Forbonnais, *Elémens du Commerce*, Volume II, chapter VIII; and in the Italian literature. F. Galiani, *Della Moneta*, book V, chapter IV, pp. 301-4); A Genovesi, *Lezioni di economia civile*, Volume II, chapter IX and Beccaria, *Elementi di economia pubblica*. Part IV chapter 7 (which though not published till 1804 had been written in 1771-72).

or loss, that is to say, using the language of this trade, if in any year the exchange were consistently and universally *below par* or *above par*, [200] it would be possible to base a sound argument on it with regard to annual reproduction. But this is an imaginary case, and in reality exchanges result in gain with one country and loss with another, and may change each day, from which it follows that any argument based on them must be extremely unreliable. It should be remembered that, when dealers try to sent capital to a foreign country, whether to obtain supplies in good time or for other speculations of their own, the exchange of the country with that market will gain, and the annual reproduction will not therefore be increased, indeed it may be reduced. Thus, argument based on the rate of exchange is always uncertain.

XXI. OF POPULATION

The most reliable means of ascertaining the increase in annual reproduction in a nation is population increase. The human species, like all others, tends by its own organization to be self-perpetuating and to multiply. Sometimes populations are wiped out by destructive natural phenomena, floods, earthquakes and volcanic eruptions. Social intercourse between nations transmits contagious diseases and wars; even industrial activity causes loss [of life] through shipwreck, or death due to illness on long voyages or as a result of breathing the poisonous air of mines in the bowels of the earth. But in the ordinary course of events, human nature is inclined towards prodigious increase; this has been clearly demonstrated by those who have studied the subject in depth. And so, in any State where the population either does not increase or does so slowly, and not in proportion to natural fertility, it must be said that the degree of imperfection in its policy is as great as the gap between what the population is, and what it should be; unless, as I have said, there is some obvious extraordinary cause of that particular measure of sterility. Habit produces in man a love of his native soil, and keeps him so attached to it that it requires dire troubles indeed to induce him to abandon it; and the married condition is so attractive, [201] that unless it proves impossible to supply sufficient marriage partners, every citizen is led by his own nature into the state of marriage.

Everyone will recognize that the strength of a State must be measured by the number of well-nourished people who live in it, and that the more populous a nation is, the greater must be its domestic consumption; and the greater this is, the more vigorous must be its annual reproduction Consequently, from the increase or diminution of the population, the growth or decrease of annual reproduction will be known; indeed, since multiplication is proof of the comforts and security people find in the State, and since the two are inseparable in societies rendered civilized through vigorous industry and rapid circulation, I say that, in consequence, the increase in population will give us the growth in annual reproduction which, rather than mere annual exports, is the measure of the strength and prosperity of a State.

The measure of the strength of a State, or its prosperity, is not always the increase in labour, as it has seemed to some,[34] because reproduction is not always proportionate to labour; indeed, in a country where the instruments of agriculture and the arts are crude and imperfect, labour will be greater, but this will not necessarily mean increased wealth or reproduction. The problem facing political economy is: *to increase annual reproduction as much as possible with the least possible labour*; in other words, given the *amount of reproduction*, to achieve it with the *minimum of labour*; given the *amount of labour*, to achieve *maximum reproduction*; to increase labour as much as possible and obtain the maximum effect from it in terms of *reproduction*. I also say that annual exportation is a questionable measure of the power and happiness of a State, since new inhabitants might be acquired, who would at first reduce annual exportation by their consumption; so that it would be possible for the number of inhabitants to increase, and exportation to fall for a few years. The truth is, however, that this would not be the [202] acquisition of solid wealth for the State, if the new consumers did not soon contribute to annual reproduction, and subsequently assist in increasing exportation. The opposite might also occur, that is to say that the population being reduced for some reason, annual exportation for a period would be increased. Exportation alone is therefore not always a safe rule for determining the state of annual reproduction.

---

[34] For an examination of English literature on this point, see E.A.J. Johnson, *Predecessors of Adam Smith*, Prentice Hall, 1937, chapter XII. This position had been criticized by the Physiocrats who argued that population or labour without adequate support from capital resources implied poverty rather than wealth. A similar position is put by Genovesi, *Lezioni di economia civile*, Volume 1, ch. 5.

XXII. OF THE SPATIAL DISTRIBUTION OF PEOPLE

Is it better for this population to be scattered throughout a vast land, or to be dense, and restricted to a smaller space? I would answer that if a population is too spread out, and scattered over a large area, domestic trade will be at the minimum possible level, because the greater the distance from town to town and from city to city, the more difficult will it be to carry out transactions. Consequently, there will be no circulation or trade except in occasional cases where there is a considerable difference in price between one place and another. The people being so isolated and distant from each other, industry cannot flourish, and annual reproduction will be limited to little more than the satisfaction of prime wants. If, on the other hand, the population is restricted to too small a space, circulation will be very rapid and annual reproduction will be at its highest level, but since the soil will not be sufficient to yield an annual production of food corresponding to annual consumption, the people will have to turn their energies mainly to manufactures, and since the value of these is dependent on men's opinions, which are capricious and change with circumstances, this value will always be more precarious and less certain than the value of the provisions from the soil which provide the nourishment for life itself. Such a dense population, then, will have an excellent annual reproduction, but its wealth will be less secure in relation to physical and natural wants. Spurred on by a high level of want to a high level of activity, a population placed in these circumstances is able to undertake and complete the boldest enterprises; but if at any time its industry and rapid circulation should [203] cease to be regulated by laws and customs, everything will immediately take on a different aspect, and only the number of inhabitants whose consumption corresponds to the annual reproduction of the soil will remain.

For a State to prosper it must be situated between these two extremes, that is to say, it must not occupy so much land that its people are removed from easy communication, and it must not restrict them so that they are forced to seek their nourishment elsewhere. A city is to a province what the marketplace is to the city: the meeting point where sellers and buyers come together. And the capital is to other cities what these are to the province.

You may ask whether it is more useful to the nation for the people to be gathered in large masses in the cities, and particularly in the capital or whether, on the contrary, it is better to ensure that this does not happen, and to prefer a population increase in country areas.

Mortality is higher in cities than in country areas, because in the more populated cities we find more intemperance, and the air is not so healthy. Added to this is the very natural reflection, that the peasant obviously contributes much more to the annual reproduction than do many inhabitants of the city. Thus, it appears that an increase in cultivators of the soil is more useful than an increase in city-dwellers.

But let us think about the principle stated earlier, that the more a population is concentrated, the greater the ferment injected into industry by a very rapid circulation. Cities, and in particular large and highly populated cities, are the meeting point producing the incentive to industry in country areas, for this cannot come out of the land by itself, circulation and wants among the people on the land being small. A large mass of people gathered in one place must spread activity into the surrounding area of land, in order to draw consumption goods from it. The conveniences of life employ a large number of craftsmen in populous cities; the arts are refined, the more difficult manufactures perfected and polished. If the same [204] population were spread out over the countryside and there were no highly populated cities, there is no doubt that circulation and industry would be less, and in consequence, annual reproduction would be lower. Everyone knows that more money is spent in cities than by those who live in the country; and everyone knows from experience that living in the biggest cities, they must purchase more things than if they lived in smaller cities. Thus the same population, distributed widely, will have less circulation, and condensed into a much smaller space, will have a much greater circulation; and annual reproduction increasing with the number of purchases, or in other words with increasing circulation, will be greater according as there are more densely populated cities in a State.

Certainly, there must exist in every State a proportion between city-dwellers and the country people. In a military State, which either stands in fear of invasion by enemies or contemplates conquests, life must be made more difficult in the city than in the country, so as to increase the cultivator, of the soil if possible, because they are the people best suited to the army, and because the more spread out a community is, the more difficult it is for an invader to take possession of it and preserve dominion over it. A million men gathered in a city will be subdued as soon as the enemy has a few artillery divisions to dominate it; the same number scattered is not so easily defeated or besieged. The Parthians, Scythians, Arabs, Tartars, the whole of history testifies to this. However, in a country which has little to fear from invasion and does not aspire to conquest, there will be no harm in having many people in the cities, for this leads to a cultivation of the land that will always be proportioned to consumption, provided the State has land that is naturally fertilizable.

A blade of perfectly ordinary grass mown on the lawn is a piece of inert material as long as it is by itself or collected into a small heap; but if we were to accumulate a voluminous mass of this cut grass, we [205] would see it begin to ferment and give off heat, so that it would finally burst into flames and light up the horizon. A bunch of grapes, as long as it is by itself or with a few similar bunches, is eventually reduced to matter that is full of sediment, but if grapes are compressed in vast quantity in containers, the impact of the infinite number of volatile particles moving against each other agitates the entire mass, and spreads effervescence through it, to distil a liquor which yields fragrant and liberating particles to the atmosphere, and brings life and youth to the veins of whoever tastes it. And that is what happens with mankind. Isolated man is timid, savage and inadequate: scattered or gathered in small groups, he can achieve little or nothing; but if a great number of men join together in a concentrated group restricted to a small space, they will become active, ferment and improve, and spread activity, reproduction and life all around them.

XXIII. POSSIBLE ERRORS IN ESTIMATING POPULATION SIZE

To return to our main argument: population growth, then, is the only sure indication of an increase in annual reproduction, as we saw in section XXI.[35] But to verify this fact exactly, a certain amount of care must be taken. Sometimes the population of a country may appear to have increased or decreased simply because of a difference in the degree of thoroughness of the research. The records kept by clerics are usually the most accurate; but if these are compared with other less exact records, the difference between the totals will not give us the state of the population. These things should not be forgotten, small though they may be, because in practice, in order to

---

[35] Above, esp. pp. 65-6.

arrive at a conclusion about population, we must be sure that the accuracy and precision of the records for each year of the comparison are, to all intents and purposes, the same.

Indeed, it would be easy, for any given nation, to prove either of the two theses—that the population had diminished or that it had *increased*—if a year were to be selected indiscriminately from the records. After a plague or the disasters of war, a country might easily have been less populous than it is today, even if the population is currently declining. In [206] calculations of this nature, two single extremes are not sufficient, but a series of several years should be selected from the immediately preceding period. In a series of six or eight consecutive years, we know what forces influenced the population; and by arriving at an average rate over several years, it is possible to find out whether the present state is in fact above or below the median; and from this a conclusion can be drawn that is more correct and proven than any other, for the purpose of ascertaining whether annual reproduction and public prosperity are increasing or diminishing.

Some curious and occasionally useful research has been done in the present century on the population of countries.[36] Nevertheless, it is true that both physical location and the laws governing each population produce so much variation in the ratios between the classes, that analogy cannot be relied upon as particularly valid. The number of clerics varies a great deal from one country to another; marriage or celibacy prevail according to the different laws and customs of the people; and so, as some distinguished writers have shown, the proportion between the sexes is variable. We must be conscious of these things in order to ensure that we reach the height of the noble art of questioning, and in order to seek truth with love and respect. Anyone establishing a ratio between celibacy and marriage, clerics and laymen, men and women, must find themselves in error in Rome if not in London.

In a comparison of populations between one State and another, the number of inhabitants of the entire country must be exactly divided by the area, which will show the number of inhabitants to

---

[36] For a general discussion of some of these population theories, reference may be made to James Bonar, *Theories of Population From Raleigh to Arthur Young*, reissued London, Frank Cass, 1966. There were also some significant Italian contributions on the subject, including a chapter devoted to the subject by Beccaria in his *Elementi di economia pubblica*, Part 1, chapter 3, pp. 401-33.

each square mile; this is the way to find out which of two States has a proportionately larger population. But if we are not to fall into any errors, we must know four things for certain. Supposing we wished to compare the population of France with that of Great Britain; we must have accurate knowledge of the following four factors: (1) the exact population of France; (2) the exact area of that kingdom; (3) the exact population of England; (4) the exact area of that island. If a single one of these is inaccurate, the calculation will be wrong.

I would be digressing too much if I were to anticipate all the possible errors in political calculations of this nature. In every State there [207] are the greens and the blues, there are those who will take advantage of public disorder and whose interest it is to embellish the present, discredit the complaints of the people and dissuade the ruler from attending to them; and there are also some ambitious men who have been passed over, and who seek to exaggerate the people's troubles out of envy of those in public office. The calculations in question must be carried out by people who love the truth impartially, and do not prefer one view to another.

XXIV. DIVISION OF THE PEOPLE INTO CLASSES

The people who make up a nation I consider to be divided into three classes: *producers, middle men* and *consumers*. I do not include the separate class of managers, such as those representing the ruler, and tribunals, judges. soldiers, ministers of religion etc.: such people are destined to guide and protect the activities of others, and their offices do not fall directly into the sphere of things which are the subject of political economy. The *producers* then, are those who work with the products of the soil, or in those arts and trades which modify what the soil produces, who in a manner of speaking create a new value, the total of which is called *annual reproduction*. The *middle men* constitute a class positioned between the producer and the consumer, who procure for the former a convenient market for the particular commodity reproduced by his industry, and offer the prompt acquisition of a corresponding amount of universal commodity; while to the latter they offer particular commodities, and the convenience of being able to choose quickly from a selection of different qualities of the same material gathered together. These middle men are all the merchants, all those who purchase for resale, all those employed in transportation, all those who are part of the means of bringing the consumer to the producer, thus facilitating circulation by the work they do. The third class of *consumers* it will be easily seen, consists of those who do not put back any of their own industry into the common mass of society, and this is their [208] distinguishing feature.

These three original classes are not, however, inherently incompatible; for indeed, every seller must be a purchaser, as we saw in section V;[37] thus every producer must of necessity be a consumer of the entire portion destined for his subsistence: and I say the same for the middle man. The consumer at first glance appears to be a useless burden on the State, because if the entire mass of those who are merely consumers were to leave the country, this would not appear to produce any effect other than an evident increase in annual exportation of an amount corresponding to the diminished domestic consumption; from which the State would gain an increase in overall circulation.

In politics, however, one must mistrust conclusions arrived at from the first appearance of things. The consumers are largely the owners of property; their idle and passive existence requires constant stimulation through the satisfaction of a variety of pleasures; they have a perennial need of money; hence they must indirectly contribute to the annual reproduction of the land; they must invent and perfect ways of increasing the annual reproduction of their property; they must serve as a continual spur to the farmer, without which agriculture would decline considerably: the thoughtlessness and prodigality of the landowner, although in certain cases harmful, is on the whole helpful to annual reproduction.

It would be a notion of Platonic perfection to imagine there were no mere consumers in a State. Those who acquire wealth legitimately must be allowed to enjoy it; and if this is the case, then there must also be some people permitted to remain idle. This group, not having to look to its sustenance and to comforts it already possesses, is the best source of magistrates, men of letters and leaders, young people who have not lacked the means for education, and to whom it is not necessary to contribute [209] for their public services the price that must needs be paid to those who have only their wages to live on.

Those consumers without possessions, who live by either pestering or cunning, begging their food, weigh heavily on the State. They represent a real additional tax burden on other industrious citizens,

---

[37] Above, pp. 19-20.

and produce no effect other than that of reducing annual exportation. The lawgiver will always contrive to reduce their numbers. I shall not enter into odious enumeration of the classes of people in this condition, but shall limit myself to a general view of my topics, leaving to others the task of applying them to practical cases. Suffice it to recall what one distinguished writer has wisely observed, that not all political vices are moral vices, nor all moral vices political ones.[38]

The three classes of men we have been speaking about would find their just proportion in the State, if the laws and opinions introduced there did not prevent things from taking their natural course; for the middle men must necessarily be restricted by the number of transactions, that is to say, by the quantity of goods produced and consumed; the producers would increase naturally until they reached the point where consumption was balanced; and so everything would inevitably be levelled out as a general consequence of needs. But where either the number of middle men is limited by being restricted to a separate class and guild, as previously described,[39] or there appears a class of consumers who possess nothing, this beneficial equalizing and harmonious relationship will be altered; and a skilled minister will always endeavor indirectly to weaken these craft institutions, putting everything as far as possible into the hands of benevolent and discerning Nature.

It is desirable for the class of consumers who own land to multiply as much as possible; for as we said in section VI, a vast expanse of land in the possession of one man will always produce less than it would if divided among many; for greater care and pains will be put into increasing the production of the soil by an owner who must make something of a mediocre parcel of land, than by a wealthy owner of vast properties who, as well [210] as having less incentive, could not, as we said earlier, watch carefully over them all.[40] Added

---

[38] It is difficult to identify this distinguished author with any certainty, but Verri may have been thinking of a number of people, including Machiavelli, Mandeville and Rousseau. See for example, Machiavelli, *The Discourses*, Bk. 1, Discourse II (Penguin Classics. edited by Bernard Crick, London, 1983, pp. 139-42); Bernard de Mandeville, "An Inquiry into the Origin of Moral Virtue," in *The Fable of the Bees*, edited by F.B. Kaye, Oxford, at the Clarendon Press, 1924, Vol. I, esp. pp. 41-42; cf. Vol. II, "The Sixth Dialogue," pp. 273-76, 280-84; J. Rousseau, *The Social Contract*, Book II, ch. 12, (Penguin Classics, translated by Maurice Cranston, London, 1971, pp. 98-100).

[39] See above, for example, section VII, pp. 24-5.

[40] Above, esp. pp. 21-2.

to this, the more owners there are of a piece of land, the more hands will be holding the products, and thus the number of sellers will be increased, to the benefit of public plenty. The methods adopted by the wise lawgiver, in this case, will be the same as set out earlier with reference to States afflicted by the evil of too much inequality in the distribution of wealth. A further observation may be made in this respect, which is, that according as landowners multiply, so will the number of those involved in the preservation of the State be greater; because those in possession of landed property are the true natives of a country, the citizens most attached to the soil, for they are made so both by reason of habit, which they have in common with every other citizen, and even more by the need to preserve their wealth and their estate, possessions which the reproducer and the middle man may easily find, even though they may change countries.

I hope those charitable and enlightened readers who have studied, and are well aware of, the sacred rights of the individual, will not scorn me if I leave those rights aside, and look only at the individual as an element of society contributing to its wealth and strength. No, I am not degrading man to the inferior condition of a mere asset; if only my voice could thus usefully proclaim the venerable original rights of intelligent and sensitive beings, which joined together, could not but improve the quality of life, rights broadcast far and wide by outstanding men who are hated by those in power, unknown to the masses, and honored by a few powerless, scattered souls whose habit it is to meditate! They should know that, as I write, I can scarcely restrain the impulse of my heart; alas cold reason advises me to promote the good of men not in the language of sentiment, but by calm analysis of things, and by enlightening those who can do some good, showing how common interests coincide. Let us respect the nobility of genius and the great virtue of him who, as a private individual, rises in loud protest against abuse of power, and endeavors to make those in positions of authority blush at their vices and their errors. If humanity were thus relieved of its ills, virtue would point out that path to us; but men's miserable condition is such that, in general, more is achieved by appealing [211] to personal interest than by invoking glory, to which rare souls alone may aspire.

XXV. OF COLONIES AND CONQUESTS

If it is true that the strength of a State and its annual reproduction are measured by, and move in line with, population, what then are we to think of colonies sent to populate distant regions to secure their conquest? For a nation whose chief strength must lie at sea, remote colonies can compensate for the damage they cause in depopulation, by their usefulness in maintaining a constant shipping activity even in peacetime; and the metropolis, by selling the products of the colonies, can provide such a spur to industry, and so increase circulation, that the number of inhabitants lost is quickly regained. But in nations whose natural strength must be on land, because the strength of those who may try to invade them is on land, and also in nations where the land is not yet populated to its natural maximum level, it seems to me that the initial depopulation caused by colonies is harmful, and that further permanent damage is caused by the obligation to maintain too great a maritime strength. I believe that no State should ever seek to build up its power in remote areas, until it has established great power in that part of the globe where it is situated. For the more it extends its external domination, the more power it takes from its internal defence. After two or three generations, the colonies lose their affection for their old homeland, and unless their population is renewed through constant sacrifice, there is a danger that they may degenerate into lukewarm allies of little use, and if they grow impatient with their dependence, they may sometimes turn into enemies.

Distant conquests bring the same problems as colonies; and if the gain in population from conquests, including those in adjoining States, is not greater than the gain in territory, there will also be the problem of having [212] to spread the population over a greater area, which will isolate men further; and we have already seen how this slows down circulation, and consequently reduces annual reproduction.

XXVI. HOW INDUSTRY IS STIMULATED BY BRINGING MEN CLOSER TOGETHER

In order to animate countries that are excessively large and lacking in population, we must be able to concentrate them only to the extent of leaving between one inhabitant and the next sufficient land to nourish them, with a desert placed between these and adjoining countries so that the peoples communicate with each other only by sea and river routes. In this way, there will be ferment and activity in the country, and population and annual reproduction will both multiply more rapidly, exportation will increase, and a new abundance of universal commodity will be acquired as a reward for industry. Moreover, since there will also be a proportionate growth in circulation and annual reproduction, it will be found that the nation gradually spreads out over the plain which it had in the first instance left deserted, until the people come into contact with their neighbors, which they will do in a condition of strength, and with the highest degree of industry and cultivation.

There is no harm in repeating, that the more isolated and distant from his fellows a person is, the closer he approaches the savage state; and conversely, the closer he moves to a state of industry and cultivation, the nearer will he be to people in large numbers; and every possible effort must be made to bring men closer to each other, to link one town with the next, and one city with the next. In this regard, it will be observed that as a government has more means to bring about this proximity, so will it be easier to accomplish this without people having to move their homes. Where taxes are imposed on transportation within a nation, the lawgiver who removes these will effectively bring closer together all the towns which were subject to the tax; but we shall come to this later.[41] Where roads are difficult and dangerous to safety, a good government, by smoothing the way and making roads easy and safe, will bring all the estates and towns using those roads for [213] communication closer together; for the expense and time involved in transporting things from one place to another, are greater in proportion to the distance, or rather to the steepness, difficulty and danger of the road that must be taken; and the reverse is equally true. The less time and expense are involved in carriage, the less price difference will be necessary to encourage transport from one place to another. And so, well made roads must increase the internal circulation of contracts and, for the reasons already mentioned, increase annual reproduction.

It is as well, however, in public works of this kind, to beware of extravagance and limit ourselves to usefulness alone; for excessively wide roads which are intended more for show than for use, are so many strips of unproductive land; and it is to be observed, that without doubt an extravagance more harmful than any other is one which prevents a useful vegetation from the soil; hence, extensive gardens, woods intended only for the ceremony of the hunt, endless avenues, and similar abuses of property, are a kind of luxury which

---

[41] Below, section XXX, pp. 97-2.

allows no recompense; for luxury in consumption leads to a proportionate annual reproduction, but this unproductive luxury directly prevents this.

On this same principle, the construction of navigable canals will contribute greatly to bringing remote populations together; the public safety of roads, suitable location of inns and other similar conveniences will, in the hands of a wise government, animate circulation, industry and reproduction in a people, as long as it is accomplished equitably. For this reason, a maritime Power whose flag is respected can be said to border on every port in the world.

XXVII. OF AGRICULTURE

Every piece of earth is the raw material of agriculture, which produces for a people the truest wealth, and that most independent of men's whims and opinions. Every type of agriculture is profitable to [214] the State, because it increases annual reproduction; but the *type of agriculture to be preferred is that which most increases annual reproduction*. The interest of the landowner would seem to be, to procure the greatest possible annual reproduction from his property; hence it would not appear to be worthwhile for the lawgiver to concern himself with it, rather he should leave it to the vigilance of the landowner's interest. This may mean that the interests of the State do not always coincide with those of the landowner. The truth of this becomes evident if we consider that the interest of the owner is not *to increase the total annual reproduction* of his property, but rather *to increase that portion of income due to himself*. That said, it will be easily seen that the income from the land may be increased in two ways, *by augmenting* annual reproduction or by *reducing* the number of day-laborers. As long as the first of these means of increasing revenue is chosen, the interest of the owner coincides with that of the lawgiver; but should the second be preferred, the interests of the State and those of the owner may be in conflict. The equations of political economy are always successfully resolved by addition, while results obtained by subtraction are always detrimental: so one must always seek the maximum action which has the maximum effect. Suppose one type of cultivation requires the labour of ten farm workers who live off the working of a field. The landowner could earn more by substituting another cultivation, which would only require two men to work it, because the saving from having eight less men to maintain could represent a larger sum than the difference between the total production of the first crop and that of the second. And so agriculture in all its aspects is something to be kept in view by those appointed to watch over the public happiness. The first general rule, then, will be: *to prefer that type of agriculture which most increases total annual reproduction and in which the greatest number of laborers are employed.*

Some kinds of agriculture can augment the annual reproduction from the land on which they are practiced, while decreasing by a far greater amount the annual reproduction of other properties. An example of this [215] might be cultivation accomplished through irrigation. If marshy lands are brought under cultivation by draining the water, this can increase the national annual reproduction; but when a river branches out and subdivides over a vast area of land, there will be a danger of frequent fogs and hailstorms bringing devastation to other country areas, with the air becoming unhealthy and the population diminishing in consequence. The evaporation of the water does not occur in relation to its absolute quantity, but in proportion to its surface area. Reason and experience teach us that rains, mists and hailstorms are far more common in countries where there is much irrigation than they are in dry countries. All things being equal, in lowlands which are similar, and similarly placed in relation to nearby mountains, the amount of rain falling each year, and the number and force of storms, are greater where rivers are scattered and divided for irrigation purposes. In Tuscany, as in Lombardy, there are surrounding mountains, yet many more hailstorms and rains occur in Lombardy, where among the Milanese there are also reliable observations that the main mists have begun as early as autumn, and that they have occurred closer to the hills, and spread in that area, with the expansion of irrigation. Second general rule: *The kind of cultivation which is detrimental to climatic conditions can always be avoided.*

There may be a type of cultivation which increases annual reproduction without loss or damage, but which exhausts the soil, so that after a few years it is rendered unproductive or too difficult to cultivate. In this case too, the nation's interests would be opposed to those of the landowner. Many countries which history tells us were highly fertile, are now only masses of barren sand. Perhaps irrigation, lapping the growth layer of the soil over many years, imperceptibly acts on the minerals and oily parts of the soil, which constitute its fertility, and dissolves them, leaving over the course of centuries land that is exhausted, dead; and as the soil is approaching this extreme it begins to need the irrigation which alone would, [216] in the first instance, have led to reproduction. The landowner does not foresee this deterioration, nor does his interest take it into account, for it is too remote, and he will not experience its consequences; immortal politics, however, thrusts its sights into the future, and teaches us that reproduction which is detrimental to the fertility of the soil is not useful to the State. And so the third general rule is this: *to prefer the kind of agriculture by which the productivity of the soil is preserved.*

Anyone can see that it is preferable for the State to obtain its immediate food needs from its lands before anything else, and that food of prime necessity is far preferable to that merely for pleasure. If the American people were to use all their land to cultivate sugar, because the total value to be obtained from it is greater than it would be from grain, I say that nation would always be dependent on foreign nations, and its life would be precarious, and before anything else it ought immediately to secure its physical nourishment from its own soil. Thus the fourth general rule is: *to prefer the kind of cultivation which satisfies physical necessities, at least until their satisfaction is generally assured.*

There are other observations to be made about agriculture, from which further precepts may be drawn. In my opinion it is more useful for the State, if what is due to the landowner is paid by the tenant in provisions, rather than in money, because in order for the tenant to amass the amount due, he must quickly sell the products of the soil; and since every nation has stipulated time periods for making rent payments on lease, sellers are likely to increase all at once, so that speculators could well appear and monopolies be created. Furthermore, a sizeable part of the money would stagnate, while the tenant was saving the amount to be paid, and thus a portion of universal commodity would be withdrawn from circulation. If, on the other hand, the owner of the property is paid with so many bags of grain or barrels of wine, etc., these inconveniences will not occur. Consider also, that the surplus of annual reproduction over domestic consumption will always be more [217] easily transported to foreign countries according as the provision is smaller in volume and less perishable; from this it becomes apparent which other rules of agriculture may be added.

However, when I say that these things are worthy of the lawgiver's attention, and that one crop should be promoted and another restricted, I do not mean to say that in any circumstances I believe it to be good to *force* landowners by direct and penal laws to select or reject one crop rather than another; nor when I outline the problems produced by too much irrigation, am I suggesting that lands not suited to another kind of cultivation should be forced into it, or prohibiting any use of lawns, or excluding that kind of agriculture from the rural economy. I am saying that type of crop is never *preferable* to the cultivation of grains; but at the same time I say, that coercive laws can never produce a single good effect; because by limiting the right of ownership through restrictions that are too narrow, they tend to intimidate people, discourage industry and reduce demand for agricultural land, and to bring about an air of depression instead of letting life blossom and activity prosper. A greater spread of the cultivation which most increases reproduction in the State will be achieved steadily, and by peaceful means, if the lawgiver indirectly invites cultivation of the most useful crops, either through a light tax on lands where such a crop is grown, or by permitting less restricted trading of the provisions produced from the most useful cultivation, or else by relieving these foods of export and general excise duty and augmenting such duties on products derived from less useful cultivation. If restrictions imposed upon the trading of grains were to force a nation into increasing its irrigation and the manufacture of cheese, this incentive could be removed by restoring the grain trade to its original freedom; man's nature is such a contrary thing, that it requires a gentle invitation, and guidance without coercion, if a constant benefit is to be obtained without being counter-balanced by some greater evil. In enlightened countries, the people advance in a direct line and the laws move obliquely; [218] but the fewer luminaries there are in a population, the more will the laws move in a direct line and the people obliquely.

Rewards can sometimes be used to help industry along, even in agriculture, and some countries give us examples of this; but in general their actual utility is small. In the first place, there is a danger that they will be issued more according to bureaucratic whim than for considered merit, and nothing debases merit more than an arbitrary distribution of rewards. Secondly, if their value is in material wealth, they will surely give offence everywhere for their uncertain and incomplete usefulness; if the value is not in material wealth, their distribution will become a gamble, and in a vigorous country the award ceremony will run a considerable risk that the seriousness which encourages emulation will be lacking. Lastly, every crop which does not achieve the essential reward of profit from sales will always be an ephemeral cultivation of very little usefulness. I am not saying that the proposed reward may not be a good thing in some cases; I say only that such things are a true luxury in legislation, which cannot be entertained until such time as the lawmaking mechanism is perfectly molded and conforms with the society for which it is set up.

We have said that the lawgiver will seek to promote one type of cultivation above another; and now, narrowing down the preferred cultivation to a single theory, I shall describe it as follows: *that which most constantly increases the total value of annual reproduction*. A diplomatic minister will never encourage any other; and once the physical necessities are assured, he will not be concerned whether the crop is spoiled or not, whether it produces many raw materials for the arts, whether there is sufficient growth for the comforts of life, for all this finds its own level; everything that is sought has a price, and the more there are who seek it, the higher the price; and if the owner of the land does not cultivate a given product, it is a sign that he gets greater value from some other use of the land, which enables him to obtain the desired raw material from other countries. The notion of forming a digest of the whole world within one's own boundaries is never an auspicious one: to increase annual reproduction and push it as far as possible, [219] unleashing and invigorating human activity—this is the sole aim of political economy.

XXVIII. SOME POSSIBLE ERRORS IN ESTIMATING THE PROGRESS OF AGRICULTURE

I have said that reproduction must be pushed *as far as possible*; I do not say take it *to its peak*, because in practical terns annual reproduction never reaches this. The movement of industry is like any other moving force; rapid though it may be, it can always receive new impetus to increase it. Speaking precisely, I know that it is a matter of finite factors, but their limit is so far removed from the current state of every country in Europe that it may be considered as infinitely distant. Let us look at agriculture alone, which is our subject at present. As long as there are pieces of land in a State not yet cultivated, as long as there are common lands, lawns and meadows and pastures capable of taking crops which will give better value in food for more people, it must be said that there is yet much to be done in the development of agriculture. There is no land which man's work cannot render fertile, therefore it cannot be said of any part of Europe, that agriculture has reached its peak there. For this to happen, all the moorlands would need to be brought under cultivation, so that all common land would be cultivated by man; and there would be grasslands and pastures, but only as much as required for maintaining the animals contributing to agriculture, and providing for the consumption of the inhabitants. The number of animals in excess of this limit, which are reared to serve as raw material for manufactures, represent a significant reduction in the population, because the number of people a State can feed is reduced according as the *number of animals* it feeds is greater.

It was once believed that the lowering of interest by the public banks, and the fact that capital was sought by only a few people, constituted proof that agriculture in a nation had reached its peak. This, it is said, is a sign that agriculture no longer has a need to make use of capital; [220] hence it is at its peak. We will find the explanation of this phenomenon if we reflect that the revenue to be had from agriculture presupposes maximum freedom of trade in provisions; that uncommon energy is required to undertake the task of adding to the value of landed property; that man's indolence is such that he will prefer less profit easily obtained, to more profit requiring greater effort and anxiety; that where activity is not in general ferment, few people will dare to rise above the common level. Therefore, if there are no convenient and secure investments for capital with higher interest, public creditors for the most part will accept the lower rate, and leave their capital in the banks. This circumstance provides no better argument for *agriculture* than it does for *manufacturing*. Reduced interest on money promotes national industry, as we have said,[42] but it is not proof that industry is already fully active. I also said, that from the interest of money we may calculate the relative well-being of nations, but in that case a uniform reduction of interest on moneys held is understood; and so, by comparing our interest with the interest current in *other States*, we will have a measure for calculating which of the two enjoys greater happiness.

XXIX. OF THE ORIGIN OF TAXES

Taxation has a great deal of influence on annual reproduction; it

---

[42] Above, section XIV, esp. pp. 45-7.

can increase or decrease it, depending on how well it is regulated. We have seen, briefly, how a wisely applied tax can encourage domestic manufacturing, and how it can promote whichever kind of agriculture contributes most to increasing overall reproduction; I shall now state the theories which seem to me to be basic to an understanding of the origin, nature and influence of taxation on a nation's prosperity. Up to now I have touched on matters proper to *economics*; it remains for me to look briefly at matters of *finance*, which is also part of *political economy*, and this includes the [221] manner in which the wealth of the State may be increased and how to make the best use of that wealth.

Although in recent years some excellent essays have been written on tax, and the principles involved have in the main been clearly explained,[43] I believe something still remains to be done by today's writers. In order to form some idea of the need for, and the fairness of, taxation, consider that a society of men could not continue to exist if the violence and fraud that might be perpetrated by one citizen against another were to go unpunished, or if a conquering nation were to come along and destroy it. Thus, it is necessary for a section of the citizenry to be employed in defending the nation as a whole, and each individual belonging to it, against any usurpation or violence from within or without the State. A group of people which had no form of government at all would, at the first threat of invasion, have either to disperse, and leave its native soil, or to hasten haphazardly to repel the aggressor. Meanwhile, the cultivation of the soil would be abandoned, and the people would be forced through hunger to bow to necessity and give in. An internal aggressor would be fought off in the same hasty and disorganized manner, force alone would decide everything, and all would be chaos.

Thus the need arises to have a number of men destined solely to safeguard the property of every member of the State: professional men, part of whose duty it would be to repel any forceful encroachment with equal force, and part of it peacefully to safeguard the rights, and organize the defence, of every individual, to watch over public happiness in all its forms. Here we have the origins of the *rulers*, the *military*, *magistrates* and *ministers*. Reason dictates that

---

[43] Verri may have been referring here to a variety of works of which Hume's essay "Of Taxes" (*Essays Moral, Political and Literary*, pp. 356-60) and Mirabeau, *Théorie l'impôt*, may be singled out.

this separate class of men, who are neither producers nor middle men, but dedicated solely to the safety and happiness of the public, a class I call the *governing* class, should be maintained by the society whose well-being it secures and preserves. The need to have this class of men constitutes the justice of taxation, and the *nourishment* proportionate to the office of each of these men, up to the limit of *public usefulness*, constitutes the total amount of the tax. Tax is thus *a portion* [222] *of the property which each individual deposits in the public treasury, in order that he may enjoy in safety the property remaining to him.*

Hence it is in the interests of every man for taxes to be paid, and for them to be used for the benefit which led to their establishment. How is it then, that where every other law truly coinciding with the interests of the majority of men is obeyed without difficulty, and violators are punished by public disapproval, taxation laws on the contrary, even though for the most part they are equally in the interests of every individual, meet with constant strong opposition among the people, and those who cheat them never meet with public disapproval? Perhaps it happens because men's intellect is fashioned like the eye, to which small but nearby objects appear to cover gigantic distant objects; thus the immediate pain of parting with a portion of one's wealth is felt far more than the remote advantage of being secured against possible violence. Secondly, the concept of private property is far more deeply rooted in the souls of men than the general idea of the State's political organization; and as taxation is both a reduction of property and a link between the individual and the State, the individual feels himself more affected by the diminution than by the compensating bond of his relationship with the State. Nevertheless, I believe that if taxes had at all times been judiciously based, public opinion would regard them as a sacred debt; and perhaps custom would have planted in people's minds as much shame in their avoidance as there is for someone voluntarily associated with a private company who, having enjoyed his share of the benefits, is unable to pay his contribution. If custom has attached stigma and shame to anyone who does not pay his gambling debts, why is a similar punishment not inflicted on anyone who fails to pay his debts to a merchant or to the treasury? Could it possibly be because the law provides for the latter, but not for the former? It should perhaps be observed, that the abuse of legislative power in the past, and the even greater widespread abuse of [223] rendering every law uncertain and doubtful in its interpretation, have left men with a less than favorable perception of the law, and that public opinion, wherever possible, absolves him whom the law condemns. In countries where the laws are appropriate, there is more coincidence between law and custom; judgements of the courts and by public opinion will be seen to be the same. Perhaps the divergence between these two is the true measure of a people's corruption. But to indulge in these notions would take me too far from my subject.

And if I were to look at tax as a legitimate share deposited with the treasury, this too would be removed from my theme. Others[44] have examined these matters. The purpose of the present work requires me to study taxation purely in its relation to, and for its influence on, the circulation, annual reproduction, industry and prosperity of the nation.

XXX. OF THE PRINCIPLES GUIDING TAXATION

There are two cases in which taxation will cause a nation to decline. First case, when the amount of the tax *exceeds* the nation's resources and is not proportionate to the general wealth. Second case, when an amount of tax, which on aggregate is proportionate to the wealth of the nation, is badly *distributed*. In the first case there is only one remedy, and it is simple: to proportion the burden to the wealth of the nation. The second case is highly variable and very complex. Let us try to put our ideas in order, and gather all the particular cases together under appropriate headings.

A tax is wrongly assessed when it immediately falls on the weakest class of people in the State, when there is some abuse in the collection of it, or when it prevents circulation, exportation or the development of industry; in short, when it impedes those operations by means of which annual [224] reproduction is increased.

Every tax naturally tends to level out uniformly among all the individuals in a State, in proportion to their consumption. If the tax is on property, let us suppose it is paid in commodities which are distributed to the governing class mentioned above. It is true that all

---

[44] This was invariably an important theme in the Physiocratic literature where taxation was presented as a *quid pro quo* for the protective services government rendered to property. See for example, Mercier de la Rivière, *L'Ordre Naturel et Essentiel des Sociétés Politiques*, esp. Chapters I-III; Du Pont de Nemours, *De l'origine et des progrès d'une science nouvelle*, 1768, reprinted in Daire, *Physiocratie*, pp. 347-52.

the individual members of that class then cease to be buyers of the commodities, and the landholder sees a reduction in the number of buyers of his commodities, so that he is obliged to sell them, all else being equal, at a lower price, and this means he will not recover the amount paid in tax from the remaining purchase. But I say that *all else* will not remain *equal* and the number of buyers will diminish; because as a new tax is imposed on the landowners, and a new interest immediately applies, there will at the same time be a fresh need for this class to have more of the universal commodity, and so from the start the most wealthy will refrain from selling, waiting for higher prices, and the few sellers remaining active, being restricted in number, will succeed in raising prices; and since levelling will have occurred when the tax was first imposed, it will of course continue to occur as long as the tax continues to be distributed in the same form, provided all else is equal. Suppose the tax is paid in money, as in fact happens: then the governing class will form a new army of purchasers who, as we have seen, will consume more according as they have the means to consume more, and naturally in this way they will cooperate with the landowner to raise the price of provisions; thus the owner of the land will obtain compensation from every consumer for the tax he has paid in advance. If the tax is on goods and manufactures, then craftsmen and merchants will try to obtain compensation by selling their manufactures at higher prices, thus spreading the tax proportionately over their consumers. If the tax is imposed directly on the lower classes who possess nothing, and who having only themselves to rent out, live on a daily wage, the common people will of course ask for a high wage; thus, a tax always has an [225] expansive force by which it tends to level out over the greatest possible area. Seen purely from this angle, it would appear to be of no consequence whether it falls more [heavily] onto one class than another.

I said that the tax is distributed and equalized naturally on the basis of what each person consumes. To make the notion clearer, let us imagine a foreigner resident among us, who has three thousand *scudi* of credit which have come from land he owns in his own country. Suppose he spends the entire amount each year for his own needs. He must pay our country's tax on what he consumes, whether directly for himself or indirectly for members of his household; and if our taxes should go up to 17 per cent of capital value, I say that the foreigner would be contributing five hundred *scudi*[45] from his land to our country's tax. When taxes are imposed on goods coming into the city, on the sale of goods for primary consumption, on houses, and on arts and trades, as they are at present practically everywhere, it is easy to see how the foreigner must perforce contribute according to his consumption. But if the taxes in our country were imposed entirely on the landlord's portion from the land, then the path to levelling consumption would be longer; he would pay more for the goods he consumed than if there were no tax, and all the work and services for which he must pay would be proportionately dearer according to the value of the land providing food for the people working for him. Hence I believe, that if the owner of a huge property consumes very little, the amount of tax he will have paid will in fact be very small; and so the foreigner, who is staying in our country, contributes very little to his own country. This also becomes clearer when we think that the tax imposed on land, if it is constant and uniform, is more like an instant reduction of the value of property at the moment of fixing it than an annual reduction of the owner's revenue; because for contracts [226] transferring properties to a new owner after the tax is imposed, the buyer has made the purchase using his money at a given annual return and taking the amount of tax out of the property. In some States this has led to laws prohibiting landowners from staying in foreign countries; a direct law, which if on the one hand prevents the exit of money and a reduction in the number of taxpayers, on the other also does not entice families from other countries to settle, purchase land, and bring their wealth and industry into the State.

To further disperse the haze surrounding this subject, consider that the man who does not possess anything cannot pay any tax, unless he seizes money from someone who does. An owner, whether of land or of capital, or some other source of money, if he maintains workers will be obliged to pay the tax imposed on them, since if he consumes their time and labour, he must give them the means to feed themselves and to pay their debt to the treasury. I say the same of the wage-earners paid by this owner, whose taxes he surely pays; and I say the same of all the goods consumed by the owner, for which he is obliged to pay the merchant the original price plus transport costs, plus the said merchant's food costs, plus the tax

---

[45] More correctly, 510 *scudi* (17 per cent of 3000 *scudi* capital value).

previously paid by the merchant. Hence, according to his consumption, every owner will pay a greater amount of tax; and the greater his tax burden, the more will he try to make up his losses with sales, and this is how tax tends to balance itself out over goods consumed. It must be kept in mind that a landowner who has bought his estate on the basis of a 3۴ per cent net return, recovers the entire return of his capital from the land, and as owner will not pay taxes; just as, whenever we acquire a landholding that is subject to an easement, we are not giving up anything of our own when allowing anyone having the right to use it, to do so. The same thing happens when paying a land tax imposed in former times. The notion that the ruler is co-owner of properties does not seem to me to be valid, and if it were, it would also hold for the warehouses where goods are stored. Everyone, then, pays tax as a consumer, because each person will [227] pay the amount of tax which is added to the cost of what he consumes, so that for a certain amount of money spent, the quantity of particular commodities he acquires for consumption will be reduced by the amount by which the price is higher due to tax; and this difference in commodities acquired will be the portion of *property* deposited in the public treasury. *For everyone knows that by the term property is meant every piece of land, commodity or good, the control of which is in our possession.* He who consumes more, pays more in tax; and tax, as I have said, is diffused and equalized over goods consumed.

Thus it appears at first glance, since tax tends to balance out over goods consumed, that the selection of one class of people over another is arbitrary; but this is not so, since this balancing out and assessment of tax is always a condition of war between one class of men and another. When the owner and the citizen in possession of land must pay tax in advance, the reapportioning among the common people is done quickly and with few obstacles, because it is the powerful asserting authority over the weak; but when the tax falls directly on the weak class, the reapportioning comes about gradually, but with the slowness or the obstacles that are inevitable when the poor and weak seek authority over the rich and powerful. These intervals between upheaval and calm are the greatest crisis that can occur in a State, and need to be studied every time a tax is altered.

The time elapsing between the imposition of a tax and the evening out (of its burden] is a time of battles and turmoil. What I say about the tax also applies to debasing the value of coins.[46] In this interval of time between the impulse given by the lawmaker and the eventual equilibrium, the class of people charged with the tax in advance bears a heavier burden than that of the normal tax; the weaker and poorer is the class chosen to carry this burden, the more evasion and declining industry are to be feared. The first criterion governing tax will therefore be; *that it never falls directly on the poor class.*

Some have thought that every tax should end up by being a "capitation" and on this principle it was imagined that the simplest thing would be to [228] tax every member of the population equally. The line of reasoning followed is this: every man enjoys manufactures and the services of poorer citizens according to his wealth, and is obliged to pay for those serving him not only sufficient food for the time they are working for him, but also the tax proportioned to that same time period, which they have had to pay. As a result of this, the capitation balances out by itself, and at the end of every year each person will have paid tax according to the degree of comforts he has enjoyed, and the common people who own nothing will have been fully compensated. Set against this argument however, is the time required for the balancing, that is to say, the interval of time during which the poor have to fight the rich. And to all this we must add the hostility such a tax inevitably brings with it, and the hateful servitude to which it degrades the people: for when a tax has as its base either the person's property or his commodities, it is something which falls on the thing and not on the person, so that the penalty for not having paid it will at most be loss of the land or goods; but when the tax falls on the person himself, it mortgages his freedom and his personal life, and the poor and powerless are affronted and oppressed by the very laws whose establishment is required to relieve and defend them. Even the most remote corners of the State, every wretched hut, must be visited by the tax gatherer; if the family of a poor peasant does not have the money to pay, an insensitive exactor will bring it to the point of destruction, the excise men will grab hoes

---

[46] In this one and only reference to the frequent practice of 'raising the value of money,' Verri appropriately compares it to taxation. As Monroe, *Monetary Theory before Adam Smith*, pp. 235-44 implies, Verri is unusual among his Italian contemporaries for not dealing with this subject at some length. However, earlier he had treated it in his *Dialogo sur disordine della moneta nello Stato di Milano nel 1762* in Custodi, Vol. XVI. pp. 279-94 and his *Consulta riforma delle monete dello Stato di Milano*, in Custodi, Vol. XVI, esp. pp. 305-7.

and spades by force; and a simple, good-living but poor family will be left in utter ruin. This must be the scene wherever there is a tax based on assessment by capitation. Wherever it is the person who pays, rather than the owner, civil liberty is fundamentally violated. The moral precepts of the nation are at risk, because continuing examples of the use of public [229] force on the innocent will destroy it. Industry will become corrupted at its roots, and the nation will never have an incentive to increase annual reproduction, because the terrifying lash of the law whistles around the heads of the demoralized producers. To these evils another is added, and that is the expense of collecting this tax, for to extract it in this form requires the maintenance of a sufficient number of officials to cover the entire land, and an annual visit to even the remotest dwelling in that State.

The costs of tax collection are purely a burden on the State, for two reasons. One is that, once the tax corresponding to the needs of the State has been paid, the cost of collecting it must also be met. The other is that, the more tax collectors of all kinds there are, the larger is the class of people who, being neither reproducers nor middle men but merely consumers (and consumers moreover who do not own land and do not defend the State), are simply dependents of the State. The natural distastefulness of their duties, their tendency to suppress any hint of compassion, and the schemes they sometimes contrive to take advantage of some real or imagined illicit trafficking, generally mean that this class of people must be as limited as it can be. Thus, the second rule concerning tax is: *to choose the form involving the least possible expense of collection.*

Tax is directly harmful to the lowest classes, not only where the capitation is open and public, but also where it is concealed or implicit. Examples of this are any taxes imposed on essential goods; and an even worse case is that of the ruler who appropriates exclusive ownership of certain goods in order to sell them only to the common people. Since these essential goods are consumed by rich and poor alike in more or less equal proportion, it is clear that such a tax in effect becomes a capitation.

Such capitation, albeit concealed, even though it implies some conflict in its equalization between the weak and the powerful, is not as odious and hostile in its execution as true capitation, because some degree of freedom always remains with the taxpayer, and also because its surety for the [230] treasury is not man's mere existence, but his indispensable needs.

Tax falls directly on the most powerless of the people when it is imposed on the smallest transactions in particular. In some countries, trade in large quantities of certain goods for public use is free, whilst the same goods cannot be sold in smaller amounts for the daily requirements of the ordinary people unless a separate tax is paid. As a result, the poorest and most needy, who at any one time never have capital to buy all they need for several weeks' consumption, sometimes end up paying with their small daily purchases as much as double the amount paid for the same goods by the wealthier. Everyone will be conscious of how little humanity and justice there is in this manner of distributing tax, and how all these burdens, the first impact of which is felt by those who own nothing, tend to discourage industry and distress the hardest working section of the population. Consequently, it will be seen that some other method of distribution of these taxes may always be found which will be of benefit to the State.

I said above[47] that the second error in tax distribution occurs where there are abuses in the collection of it. It is an abuse of tax collection if in the class of people charged with [the public] finances there is excess in numbers or in wages paid; for as has been noted, the burden of this falls on the people. The problem to be solved every time tax is under discussion is this: *how to ensure that there is the least possible difference between the amount paid by the people and the total amount on the treasury's books, while allowing as much freedom as possible to the nation.*

It is an abuse in the collection of tax, and a gross one, when there is scope for arbitrary decisions to be made, and the financiers [of the tax farm] can exempt some people and overburden others at will, so that those who are weak and isolated are placed in a position of having either to put up with an unjust use of power against them, or to institute a lawsuit against a powerful person charged with collecting taxes who has easy access to the courts. Whenever it happens in a society that man has more power than the law, there can be no hope of industry. For industry does not reign unless there is security of person and property in general throughout the land, nor [231] will industry ever be seen to animate a population if it is not accompanied by civil liberty, so that by the sacred authority of the

---

[47] Above pp. 89-90 and cf. the earlier remarks against tax-farming in Section VII, p. 27 above, and below, p. 91

law, every member of society receives such protection, that no one can ever appropriate his possessions with impunity. And so, the third rule of taxation is: *that the laws governing it should be clear, precise and inviolate, and observed impartially with regard to every taxpayer.*

The third error in tax assessment is when it is directly opposed to circulation or to growth in annual exports, in other words when it stands in the way of any action which is useful to the State in encouraging increased annual reproduction. As indicated previously,[48] every tax imposed on the carriage of goods from place to place within the State, has the same effect as physically removing one place from the vicinity of the other; hence, it tends to reduce transactions and the circulation. Every tax imposed on the right of transit through roads and the carriage of goods, such as tolls, transport duties and duties on carriage etc., is of this nature, and has the same effect of dispersing the people in a nation, isolating its parts and reducing communication between them. These evils, as anyone can see, concern *circulation*, that is to say the country's internal transactions. It is sometimes useful to turn away a foreign buyer, and at other times a foreign seller, and this is the effect of taxes on commodities, to be discussed in section XXXIV;[49] but it is never useful, indeed it is harmful, to separate one man from the next, one village from the next, or the domestic buyer from the local seller, as we have seen. And I repeat here that my *ideas* are all inter-connected and form a whole.

Similarly, internal circulation will be hampered by any tax imposed on transactions because, although it does not directly prevent the carriage, it does however slow down rapid communication between people, reduce the number of transactions, lower circulation, and consequently, tend to reduce annual reproduction. The fourth rule therefore is: *never to arrange taxation so that it directly increases the costs of transportation from one place to another* [232] *in the State, or intervenes between the domestic seller and the domestic buyer.*

If it is desired to impose a tax on the entry of raw materials into the country for use in national industry, or on instruments used by that industry for manufacture, it is obvious that the annual reproduction of manufactures will decline; similarly, if a tax is imposed on the export of local manufactured goods from the State, there is a danger

---

[48] See above, section XXVI, esp. p. 76.
[49] Below, pp. 101-4, cf. above, pp. 75-7.

that they will take second place in competition in other countries because of their excessive price, unless the excellence of the products is such that they have no competitors.

If by increasing the value of his land through industry, spreading agriculture to previously uncultivated land, or procuring more farmers to work at his craft—in other words, if in proportion to the effort he makes to improve his situation by his own industry—a man brings upon himself a proportionately greater tax burden, then that tax is diametrically opposed to progress in industry and will contribute directly to preventing the development of annual reproduction. Hence, the fifth rule: *a tax must never be made to follow hard on the heels of growth in industry.*

There is no need for me to remind my readers that any taxes imposed upon marriage are harmful, because they are a direct obstacle to population growth.

It may further be observed, that if the tax is paid once or twice a year, and either is not divided, or is divided into a small number of portions, it will come about as the time approaches to pay it, that a vast amount of money will be removed from circulation, indeed there will be a need to begin putting it aside some time beforehand, so that in forced movements a considerable amount of the universal commodity will be withdrawn from the making of transactions, and trading activity will be slowed down. Therefore, the greater the number of small payments the tax can be divided into, the more uniform will the movement of circulation remain.[50]

XXXI. VARIOUS FORMS OF TAXATION [233]

I have indicated which form of distributing taxation I believe to be harmful to a nation. Let us briefly note the various guises in which the people may be presented with taxation.

Some are visible, and these include any payments made by citizens to the public treasury for which they receive nothing directly in return. Also included are taxes paid by an owner on his land, by a merchant on his goods, by the master of the house on his dwelling, by the traveller in tolls, and by anyone as a capitation.

Others are hidden taxes. Included in this category are a ruler's

---

[50] This rule conforms to Verri's strong anti-hoarding sentiments and his belief in the virtues of maintaining a satisfactory monetary circulation. Cf. above, section XVII, esp. pp. 53-4.

right to exclusive sales of salt or tobacco or any other goods; for while the citizen pays the tax, he also purchases the commodity, and the amount of the tax is almost amalgamated with and concealed in the natural price of the commodity he is buying. Such are also, all taxes paid in advance by the trader on behalf of the consumer at the time foreign goods enter the country, taxes which the purchaser pays almost without realizing it, because they are absorbed into the price of the goods. If anyone doubts that the consumer must pay these, let him consider that the trader wants to get from the sale his food needs, plus a profit, as we saw in section III;[51] and that the foreign manufacturer will not lower the price except in the extremely rare event of his not finding a market for his goods in our country. As soon as a trader is no longer compensated by the purchaser for tax he has paid in advance, and is obliged to subtract it from his fixed profit, he will turn to some other kind of trading. If the foreign manufacturer were in this situation he would turn to some other kind of work, and as soon as a tax on goods is not paid by the purchaser, that area of trading is wiped out.

There are two further subdivisions of tax with respect to the State: some taxes are *compulsory* and some *voluntary*. Those on land and those based purely on capitation, on houses, etc. are compulsory; because any citizen who wishes to remain in his country is not at liberty to exempt himself from these. Taxes to which a man submits by choice in order to obtain some [234] benefit are, or at least appear to be, voluntary. First among these is the tax on lotteries. I am not referring to every kind of lottery without distinction; there are many evenly balanced between risk and profit; but some lotteries conceal such injustice, that had this kind of tax not become traditional during the last century, such is the degree of humanity at present reigning in Europe, so much progress has been generally made by reason, so enlightened is the recognition of the relationship between the public interest and the protection of the common people, that I dare believe that if this idea were being proposed now for the first time, it would be rejected. One would not wish to see the venerable authority of laws, drawn up to ensure the fairness of contracts, debased to the point of becoming an insidious invitation to ingenuous citizens, with contracts so seductive and so damaging that, were they to be made with far less inequality between private

---

[51] Above, for example, p. 10.

individuals, they would be disallowed by these very same laws. The lowest among the common people, who as a general rule are never, nor ever can be, particularly shrewd or calculating, are deceived through enormous, fanciful hopes of a highly improbable fortune, for which the poorest families in the land sacrifice their beds and the clothing of their wives and children, and are reduced to the ultimate misery and desperation. Superstition, crimes, theft, prostitution and all kinds of immoral practices are encouraged by this category of voluntary tax, which has at times been used as a means of seduction by the most virtuous of men, fathers of the people, even lawgivers. I repeat, that I do not speak indiscriminately of all lotteries; I refer only to those which entice the poorest of the populace into a contract out of all proportion, the injustice of which would be greeted with amazement if the complicated calculations and the fog surrounding the extremely disproportionate risk were easily penetrable by the authorities. And so I say, that this category of tax, even though voluntary, would be less harmful if distributed throughout the nation in some other way, which is the more easily achievable since it is never a [235] major area of revenue for the treasury.

XXXII. OF THE CLASS OF MEN AMONG WHOM TAXATION IS BEST DISTRIBUTED

How then can public taxes be shared out with the least harm to the people? The answer emanates from the five rules stated above.[52] Taxation is less harmful to the State if it does not strike directly at the poorer classes, if its collection is less expensive and less subject to abuse, if it does not directly increase the costs of domestic transport, or intervene between seller and purchaser, and if its increase follows not too closely on the heels of growth in industry

It was indicated earlier[53] that tax always represents a law which induces a certain number of people to evade it. Thus a tax will always be more constant and secure when the number of people on whom it falls directly is small. There will be two advantages in this: the advantage of having to keep an eye on fewer debtors, and the advantage of lower collection costs, these being lower as the number of direct taxpayers diminishes.

Given that this is the case, which group of citizens can the State

---

[52] That is, in section XXX; summaries of the rules are given on pp. 88, 89, 91 and 92 respectively.

[53] See section XXIX above, esp. pp. 83-4.

select with least harm to pay it direct tax? The *owners*' class. Owners are people who control and own land, or houses, or merchandise, or universal commodity given out on loan or in public or private banks. Justice dictates that each of these four categories of owners should uniformly, and according to the property they own, bear all the nation's burdens directly, because they draw from society not only the protection of their person, in common with every other citizen, but also that of their real property; and as those [236] who do not possess money cannot give any to the treasury, it is reasonable that the treasury should receive a portion of the annual reproduction from the hands of those who own it.

We saw earlier[54] the power taxes have to spread, and how owners attempt to share out the load and involve also those who do not own anything by means of more intense and active industry, which is the only basis on which those without possessions can contribute their part of the tax. Besides, the owners are the only class who can pay the tax in advance, for they alone have the power to do so, and moreover they alone can reapportion it swiftly, and by means of their consumption spread the burden of public dues.

I have said that justice dictates that the four categories of owners should pay without discrimination, according to the property they own; but in politics necessity often requires that we diverge from strict geometric precision, and it is wise to turn away from that great enemy of good, that which appears to be best. It is not just a matter of avoiding every disadvantage or partial injustice (for taxation always has some of these); it is simply a matter of choosing the lesser disadvantages, and no more than that.

How are those who have universal commodity on loan to the people, or in the public banks, to contribute to taxes? With the public banks it is an easy matter; but why pay out interest and then reduce it? It would be far simpler to lower interest in the manner described elsewhere.[55] How can interest paid by private people become the basis for taxation? Shall we oblige every man to make his debts public? This would mean using a most odious law to reduce that not inconsiderable part of the circulation which depends solely on men's trust, and as a consequence slowing down industry. If voluntary disclosure is relied upon, taxable property will appear to

---

[54] See above, section XXX, esp. pp. 85-7.
[55] See above, section XV, pp. 48-9.

be minimal, and the ingenuous will suffer. Shall we resort to rewarding [237] informers in order to discover undisclosed interest incomes? Mistrust and suspicion will then spread among the people, and custom will be corrupted at the core. What kind of register can be made of these loans? Changing every month, indeed every day, and continually fluctuating in quantity. And with the added cost of a large number of employees needed to run after these constantly moving elements and keep a record of them, the partial injustice of leaving owners in this category exempt, and assigning their share to another area, will be found to be a lesser evil than becoming overwhelmed by this chaos of most serious disorders.

XXXIII. OF WHETHER ALL TAXES SHOULD BE ASSESSED ON LANDED PROPERTY

Farming land, houses and goods, then, are taxable. In recent years, there has been no shortage of profound writings on the subject of tax in which it is maintained with some accuracy that it must fall entirely on land, and that farming land is to be considered the only form of property taxable by the State.[56] This form of distributing taxation is in perfect accord with the five rules established above; for the initial burden would never fall on the poor, collection would be at very low cost, and there would be inviolable laws excluding any possibility of abuse; it would never interrupt circulation; nor would it penalize the growth of industry, as long as land recently placed under cultivation remained exempt from the tax law for a certain number of years. There is no simpler method than this. A general estimate of all the landed property in the State would reveal the taxable property over which taxation could be spread. It would be possible to discover every year how much money the treasury needed, how much needed to be spent by the State in maintaining public works, roads, bridges, embankments etc. (costs which are always best spread widely over the whole of society); the cost of new work needed to make rivers and canals navigable for use by industry [238] and to bring properties closer to each other, etc. All these territorial costs, added to the treasury's fixed expenses, would make

---

[56] A view of course particularly suggested in the Physiocratic literature, with which Verri was well acquainted, but going back to much earlier times. For a survey see Peter Groenewegen, *The Physiocrats, the Origins of Scientific Political Economy and the Single Tax*, First Henry George Memorial Lecture, Sydney, Macquarie University, October 1984, pp. 24-32.

up the amount to be levied on all properties shown in the land register, and so by means of a simple computation, the amount due for each *scudo* of capital value of landed properties would be established. Every property and every district would have its local register showing the total amount of *scudi* at which its land was valued, together with a detailed list of names showing the value of each field; and so by means of a simple decree, each owner would know when the time for paying his tax fell due, and how much he had to pay. Every property would have its own tax-collector, who would be obliged to pay the given amount into the provincial fund within the specified time. The tax collector would sometimes have to pay the sum in advance on behalf of one or two owners, against which he would have the fully guaranteed mortgage of the properties subject to tax, and from which he would have to collect interest on the money advanced: interest fixed by law, certainly, but at higher than current rates. The provincial funds would then make use of the tax, either forwarding it to the capital city or employing it according to orders they would receive from the government's financial authorities. Such a system has been usefully employed for distributing tax over land holdings.

However, if duties were to be suddenly abolished and tax allocated entirely to landed property, it is certain that this operation would have the effect of reducing the capital value of all land holdings, by an amount equivalent to the increase in capital, the interest on which would be equal to the newly levied tax. If 35 *lire* were to be added annually to the perpetual tax on a property, the price of that property would at that moment fall by at least a thousand lire, assuming that the investment in land is made at less than 3½ per cent; and the owner of the land, if he were to sell it, would receive a thousand *lire* less for his property. Even if, with the passing of many years and changes in the ownership of properties, society were to find itself organized with a perfectly satisfactory system, it would still remain to be seen whether it is such a good idea to completely sacrifice the [239] well-being of the present society, with daily evidence for its successful continuation, to a future society of unknown descendants. I shall never cease to condemn the thoughtlessness of our ancestors who, through many wrong dealings and public debts, caused the penalty for their abuses to fall on the present generation; yet the other extreme is equally harmful. As long as political affairs are managed by men, and trust is brought into play, along with the unknown elements that go by the name of fortune, it will always be a mistake to accept a known and appreciable evil in order to achieve a public good in some distant future, which moreover will be an uncertain quantity, because in any country, over a long period of time, unforeseen needs and circumstances will always arise.

I said in section XXX that tax is apportioned among consumers.[57] But a tax impulsively imposed on land holdings, without evaluation of the consequences, becomes a permanent binding loss on the property: it is a reduction of capital and represents a truly unproductive policy for the current owner; for if he sells the land, he will never recover his tax but will have borne it alone; if he keeps it, he can never recover his losses through the sale of the products of his soil, unless the importation of similar products into the country be prevented; an action which would be hostile to the people as a whole, and which would involve protection duties, and remove the uniform simplicity which is required when such things are proposed. Thus it seems to me, that it would be unjust to suddenly impose a significant portion of tax on landed property, abolishing other taxes, because it is unfair to impose a major share of public duties on a single class so that it cannot be spread, and because the owners of commodities also are owners, who receive from the State the same protection of their real property, and consequently they too must, in proportion to their wealth, bear some of the burden of public protection. If annual reproduction is the true basis of a nation's wealth, and if this annual reproduction is made up in part of foodstuffs and, fruits of the soil, and in part of manufactures, it will not matter whether [240] a man is rich because he possesses one rather than the other; and if justice suggests that owners be made to contribute to taxes according to their wealth, it seems obvious to me that the owner who is a trader must bear part of the burden, just as the landowner must.

If it is desired to exempt the trader altogether, and lay the burden entirely on the landowner, people will turn their industry more to manufactures than to agriculture, and there will be a danger that the evils of the tax may fall on agriculture, when its shortfall is the result of its disproportion to the strength of the taxpayers. Nor will the landowners ever be able to balance out with the State the oppressive tax imposed on them, as long as the State can obtain its provisions

---

[57] Above, esp. pp.85-7.

from somewhere else, such as another country: for should the landowner try to compensate for the tax by selling his grain, wine, oil etc. at a higher price, the trader will bring in the same provisions from another country, and force the landowner to lower his prices. Indeed, it will be observed in this regard that if the State happens to lie adjacent to a fertile country with a light tax on land, all the foreign provisions will come in without any duty being paid, and will gain preference, unless the local landowner lowers the price of the local provisions to the same level; and so the new land tax would result in a continual reduction of the landowner's wealth, both in annual income and in any sale he might wish to make of his property. In a large and sprawling nation, this would only occur close to the borders; but in a smaller country the damage would affect every area, and penetrate right to the center of the community.

Every tax paid by the farmer in food, clothing and contracts, and under any guise in which he pays in real terms, is in fact paid by the owner of the land. This is obvious; for out of the annual reproduction of the fields must come cultivation costs, the farmer's nourishment, and every tax paid by him. what is left will be the landowner's share; and if all taxes [241] are lifted from the farmer, the landowner's share can be increased by an equivalent amount. Thus the farmer's tax falls on the property-owner. I say the same of the tax paid by every domestic in the pay of the landowner, for he who owns nothing in this world other than his wages, takes from these the means to pay his tax; and so the landowner can be relieved of as much of the tenant's share as has been added to his own portion; and he may similarly be relieved of as much of the wages of his servants as they take in the form of consumption, and so may the manufacturer reduce the remuneration of his workers by as much as they consume. Therefore, by transferring the whole of the tax previously paid by farmers and employees to the landowner's share, two excellent ends will be achieved: the income for the treasury will be made more secure and free of problems, and the landowner himself, the cultivators and the employees will all have been relieved of the abuses and major expenses involved in collecting the former tax.

Remember, however, that one fifth of any country's population lives in the cities, and although this proportion (which was put forward by one of the first writers to reflect upon several of these matters) has been challenged by an English philosopher, it will in practice generally be found correct.[58] Of the four-fifths who live outside the cities, a considerable proportion do not live by agriculture, but rather by trading. The proportion living in the cities is certainly not entirely made up of landowners and their employees. There is a sizeable group of citizens who own goods, and many others employed by these; and the total amount of the tax which the owners of goods and their employees actually pay would, if it fell on the land, place too heavy a burden on the property owners and represent a physical and actual reduction in their wealth.

If the entire tax were on land, it is also true that the landowner would receive some relief by way of his own consumption of food and clothing and adornments, livery, horses and their maintenance, etc., because he would have to spend proportionately less on these things according to the tax they incurred, the cost of its collection, and the arbitrary application [242] of it. But is this gain comparable to the overburden that would fall to his share as landowner? A balance will come about, if the reduced collection costs are equal to the tax formerly paid by all the citizens neither owning land, nor being farmers nor employed by landowners.

XXIV. OF TAXES ON COMMODITIES

In addition, it should be considered that, if all taxes were to be distributed on landed property, the State would in fact lose the benefit that could come to it from a designed tariff on goods both entering and going out of the country. The tax on goods serves to deter rival nations, just as bounties serve to bring us closer to such

---

[58] Although this may be a general reference to the dispute between Hume on the one side and Montesquieu and Robert Wallace on the other (see for example, *Lettres Persanes*, Letters 106, 112, 117 in *Oeuvres de Montesquieu*, pp. 106, 112, 124-25; *L'Esprit des Lois*, Book XXXIII chapters 14-15, 17-19; David Hume, "Of the Populousness of Ancient Nations," in *Essays Moral, Political and Literary*, esp. pp. 410-11, 417, 421-23. Robert Wallace, *A Dissertation on the Numbers of Mankind in Ancient and Modern Times*, Edinburgh, 1753. esp. pp. 95-104), it is more likely to be a reference to Wallace alone. In 1769, Verri had referred to him in this context in his *Riflessioni sulle leggi vincolanti* (p. 339 n.27) and from population statistics in Milan for 1767 had demonstrated this ratio of five to one between country and city population (see *Riflessioni*, pp. 340-41, 368-69). Cantillon, it may be noted, argued "it is generally assumed that one half of the Inhabitants of a kingdom subsist and make their Abode in Cities ..." *Essai sur la nature du commerce en général*, edited H. Higgs, p. 45). Cf. Venturi, "Le 'Meditazioni'," p. 547.

other nations as required in the interests of our annual reproduction. A tax on the exportation of a raw material can be a very strong incentive to growth in annual reproduction, by converting it into a manufacture. A tax on a manufactured article from another country can encourage domestic manufacture of a similar item. I shall not elaborate on these arguments, which have been clearly explained by other writers.[59] The direction which may providently be given to industry by means of such charges, the substantial increase in annual reproduction which can be achieved with a tax wisely imposed on goods, are benefits of such importance that I believe they far outweigh the inconvenience of the collection costs.

A well-regulated tariff can thus be extremely useful in protecting local industry and encouraging reproduction in a nation; but this does not mean that I believe the tax on goods can ever induce foreign land holders to contribute to a domestic tax; for either foreign goods coming into the State will have tax imposed upon them, which will be paid by the local consumer, as we have seen,[60] or else the tax will be imposed on the exportation of our own goods, which again will be paid by the consumer in the other country, it is true, but it will never fall on landed properties. The land owner as such never pays a tax; the tax is always and inevitably paid by the consumer. It is true that, in the final analysis, the consumers are the owners, since [243] they pay all the consumption of those owning nothing (whose time they are consuming); however, they are paying the tax not as *owners* but as *consumers*. If, however, it is desired that foreign consumers contribute to tax in this manner, countries which compete with us for sales may wipe out our exportation by offering the goods at a lower price.

I believe a wisely conceived scale of charges and a tax judiciously imposed on goods to be extremely beneficial to any nation; but I do not think it is ever useful to prohibit the exportation of any raw material from a nation, though I believe it is useful to impose a tax on that exportation. The reason for this has already been indicated elsewhere:[61] because prohibitive and constraining laws on exportation lower prices, by removing all foreign buyers from local sellers at the outset. Once its price has fallen, cultivation of a raw material must be reduced, and it will fall into the hands of a few monopoly-

---

[59] See the references provided in n.17 (p.27) above.
[60] See Section XXX, above pp. pp. 85-7.
[61] See above, section VIII esp. pp. 27-8.

holders, who will not allow the nation to enjoy even the abundance of this raw material, as discussed earlier; where a tax is imposed with caution, it has the effect of turning away foreign buyers, certainly, but it does not exclude them, nor does it give rise to a monopoly.

With regard to the custodianship of this tax on goods, it may be observed that the greater the volume and the value of the goods, the higher must the tax be; because the easier it is to cheat, and the more it is in a person's interest to do so, the more cheating there will be, and the natural punishment for contraband is loss of the goods in question.

The scale of charges should be a simple, short list, easily portable, which shows in alphabetical order all the goods that are subject to tax, with the amount to be paid for each on entry and on exit. Goods merely in transit should remain exempt, because such exemption encourages a greater flow [244] through the country, and the money left behind by the carriers will more than compensate for the minor loss of the tax; for otherwise the transit tax is imposed either indiscriminately according to weight, or according to distinction by category of merchandise; if it is done indiscriminately, a hundred pounds of silk or gold must pay the same tax as a hundred clay vases, a most unjust inequality which would exclude transit of most goods of lesser value; if distinctions are made, everything which is in transit must be subjected to examination, and the owner of the goods will not tolerate their passage through a State where they must be unpacked and repacked in the presence only of the carrier, with the risk that some may be stolen or badly repacked. The risks and inconvenience of imposing a tax on transit of goods, in my view, are such that the small amount to be obtained from that meager portion of the tax does not compensate for them; and complete freedom of passage is so hospitable a policy and so in keeping with reason and public interest, that I do not believe anyone can be inconvenienced by it. Some goods are charged by *measure*, some by *weight*, others by *number*, and still others according to an estimate of their capital value. The charges should follow the usage of trade, and should be levied according to the standards used commonly in transactions. Goods which are neither weighed nor measured for contracts of sale and purchase, should be taxed according to their estimated value, because in that type of merchandise there is a big difference in capital value, even between two things with the same name. All domestic transportation should be completely free, and the tax should be uniform in every part of the State for the same type of goods. In this way, the total amount of tax would be borne by all forms of property holdings, and all commodities entering within the confines of foreign trade, so that traders would take on some of the dues for agriculture, and those in possession of universal commodity would be left free to invest it in the growth of annual reproduction, or in agriculture and manufactures, and the tax would be imposed on all assessable owners.

I have said that the tax to be imposed on goods is only assessable [245] on goods crossing the boundaries of the State—that is to say goods leaving or entering it—never among goods in internal circulation. Everyone will know what a boundary is. Sometimes the imagination creates new words before the ideas have been formed; there are *political* boundaries and *economic* boundaries, just as there are *arithmetical* budgets and *economic* budgets, and so on. Human ingenuity is more likely to have boundaries than is trade, the economic boundaries of which are the whole of the globe, as long as there is freedom.

The question has been put, whether if all nations were to reach an agreement to abolish taxation on goods, so that every commodity would be able to enter and leave a State freely and without payment of a single duty, this would be universally beneficial, or what effects it would have. Were it possible to hope for such an agreement between the powers of Europe, it is easy to foresee the consequences, for they would be the same as those that arise in a State when taxes on internal circulation are removed. The nations would move closer together; transactions would multiply; industry in general and annual reproduction would be given new life all over Europe; people would enjoy greater comforts; but the power of States, that is to say the relationships between one State and the next, would remain the same. If it were possible to hope for such a felicitous agreement (at a time when no accord has even been reached to make weights and measures conform to a general standard, something which would not involve the slightest sacrifice or expense to achieve), nobody would want to oppose such a provident and humane idea, which would contribute to increasing the number of our species and augmenting the comforts of life for every individual. But as long as other States impose taxes on commodities and endeavor to keep our goods from being consumed within their boundaries, we too will be forced to increase the price of the raw materials they receive from us, and at the same time place a tax on the domestic consumption of foreign manufactures, so that our own will as far as possible have preference;

and if any single nation were not to do this, I say that such a nation would feel the full [246] force of the troubles that taxes on goods may cause, and would have rejected the gain that is to be had from them.

To sum up the theory of tax, I shall say that while in precise terms justice requires that tax be shared out among all owners according to the amount they own, in fact the difficulties that would otherwise arise make it necessary to exclude those who merely possess universal commodity. Hence only the owners of lands and of saleable commodities are the logical people to advance the tax eventually paid by the consumer. Assessed in any other way, tax will always be a greater burden to the nation.

XXXV. THE METHOD OF MAKING USEFUL TAX REFORMS

There are few countries where taxation is so simple that only two tax collections are made, one on landed *property* and one on *customs*. How can an able finance minister unravel the intricate network of taxes, duties and privileges that crisscross an entire nation and connect the movements of its citizens? Taxation, the most interesting and sensitive part of the body politic, can never be dismantled suddenly or violently. The ancient finance systems are fabrics, gradually woven over time, with no master mind overseeing their design; they are crumbling edifices shored up by supports, and to remove them all at once would amount to causing their ruin. Extreme caution is necessary, and a tentative approach to change and improvement is called for, rather than rushing in with strong measures.

Remnants of tax assessment methods from past uncivilized eras are still to be seen. Ignorance of geometry meant that no one could imagine a map or a tax register for all the lands falling within one province; and so the basis used for apportioning tax was either the population of each estate, in which case frequent wars and plagues rendered the assessment [247] highly unequal when it was regarded as fixed; or alternatively, the annual record of crops harvested: a most costly and loathsome operation which left assessment to the discretion of clerks. This second method is older, and is perhaps more in keeping with the unsophisticated concepts of exact proportion between a person's annual rights and his annual charges, which avoided subjecting fluctuating fortunes to a constant tax burden. Moreover, taxes on goods were originally more like tolls, the charge being so much per cart or donkey load; subsequently, goods were taxed a percentage of their value, without any thought of favoring one commodity over another. Public wants increased as societies became more civilized, and a greater volume of universal commodity was brought into Europe; small nations were united, and, with the decline of the feudal system, Europe was left divided into sizeable areas, and wars were fought by substantial armies with permanent soldiers. Because of the flaws in the two registers—of landed property and duties—new taxation could not be added to them; with the result that an amazing array of highly novel taxes were dreamed up by incredibly fertile minds, particularly over the past two centuries, and many harmless and sometimes even useful actions were prohibited; new crimes emerged; people were thrown into prison; new criminal legislation and a new tax language were introduced: this is the picture the provinces of Europe currently present to reform.

Let us suppose that a minister wishes to simplify his country's finances so that there are two taxes only, *customs* and *land tax*. How shall he set about achieving this felicitous ideal in a way that is both gradual and safe? In the first place, the custom of farming tax collection, particularly where large amounts are involved, must be outlawed. Someone[62] has already observed, that the sovereign of all administrations is that of the father guiding his family's interests, and, quite apart from a dislike of quick riches, that big contractors are harmful because of the laws which indirectly they strive to promulgate. I believe also, that to bring in [248] contracts which limit the benevolence of the ruler and the wants of his people, is directly harmful to any constitution, and that riches accumulated by a company in permanent need, jeopardize the virtue of the authorities. He will set his sights on one of the less important and more loathsome taxes imposed on farmers and begin by abolishing that, replacing it with a corresponding extra tax on land. He will then take some similar tax paid by craftsmen or professional or trade guilds, and will replace it either with an increased duty, or with a general increase of so many per cent, or else a particular increase on a few items better able than others to support a higher tax. Then, alternatively returning to indirect taxes on agriculture and moving on again

---

[62] Very likely a reference to Mirabeau's *Théorie de l'impôt*, which not only was strongly critical of tax-farming but also started its discussion with passages reminiscent of Verri's views as here expressed.

to goods, he will gradually impose part of the increased tax burden on landlords' taxes, and part on duties. By temporizing in this way, he will be able to determine the effects of his operations without ever jeopardizing public peace, as sometimes happens when too much experimenting is inadvertently carried out. Humanity does not permit the learning of anatomy on living persons.

The lawgiver usefully paves the way for any salutary reform, if he ensures that the nation is enlightened regarding its real interests, and considers the happiness of the people. In the last century a mistaken policy prevailed, and peoples became poor; the treasury was overburdened with debts, and rulers lost that strength and energy which they have regained in happier times. Ruling a country at that time was defined as *the art of keeping the people obedient*. The shadow of mystery hung over all public affairs. Population, languishing trade, and the finances of a State were things of which some aspects were known to a few financiers but nobody dared, or was able, to see them as an integrated whole. The path of public investments was only trodden with misgivings, and with pretence as a travelling companion. Heaven has favored us with a rather different century! The [249] governments of Europe are now generally vying with each other to destroy the evils inherited from that erroneous policy. The art of ruling a people is known and defined as that of *reviving its prosperity*. The truths put forth by a privileged few have spread generally throughout Europe, and have ascended the thrones of benevolent rulers, intellects have been roused, and the resulting friction is spreading reciprocal light destined to clarify subjects relating to the common happiness; matters certainly worthy of our reflection, even more than are abstract truths and natural phenomena and the events of antiquity: all these boundaries, within which attempts were made in the past to confine the kingdom of reason, are too narrow.

As proof of what I say, books have been published in recent times in every country and every language, concerning public economy, trade, government and taxes; books wherein the authors have freely and skillfully put into the hands of the people, mysteries the mere mention of which in other times would have been an outrage.[63] The

---

[63] Examples from Italy would have included Genovesi, *Lezioni di economia civile*; Beccaria, *Elementi di economia pubblica*; Costantini, *Elementi di Commercio* (Genova and Venezia, 1761); in addition. Verri was familiar with Forbonnais, *Elémens du Commerce* and his rendition of Uztariz as *Mémoires et considérations sur le commerce*

question of whether or not regulations and laws regarding a number of public matters are useful, has been discussed and presented as a problem to be solved. Each member of the population can educate himself, think, and have his own opinion; nor has any harm befallen these authors, indeed many of them have been rewarded, and judged by virtue of their works to be worthy of public employment. An able minister, then, will arouse in people a curiosity to learn about financial and economic matters; will establish chairs in those subjects, so that in instructing young people, enlightened men will impress upon them the true driving principles of public happiness;[64] he will allow free entry to works which are devoted to such useful matter; will leave freedom to the press, by means of which any citizen may properly and acceptably express his opinions on public matters. In this way, through open debate and free exchange of ideas, it is easy for excellent notions to emerge, and amidst the dreams and the nonsense are sometimes sown seeds that prove most useful to the prosperity of the State.

The more enlightened the public is, the fairer judge it will be of the good emanating from the throne, the more responsive to reason, and grateful for that which the sovereign provides. In a civilized society, there will be no whispering of malicious rumors to intimidate ministers as soon as they make a move to remedy an old sickness in the community. We know from history how hard the Sullys and Colberts of this world must have had to battle for many years.[65] To

---

et les finances d'Espagne (Amsterdam, 2 volumes, 1761) and his Principes et observations oeconomiques (Amsterdam, 2 volumes, 1767); J.F. von Bielfeld Institutions Politiques, ouvrage ou l'on traite de la société civile, des loix, de la police, des finances, du commerce, des forces d'un État (Paris, 4 volumes 1762) as well as Physiocratic works of which Mercier de la Rivière, L'Ordre Naturel et Essentiel des Sociétés politiques was the most important in this context.

[64] The Austrian government in Milan had established such a chair in 1769 which was filled by Verri's friend, Cesare Beccaria. In 1754, the University of Naples had established a similar chair for Antonio Genovesi.

[65] A reference to Maximilien de Béthune, Duc le Sully (1559-1641), the Prime Minister of Henry IV and Jean-Baptiste Colbert (1619-1683), the Finance Minister of Louis XIV. Combining these together may have been a deliberate taunt at the Physiocrats, of whose doctrines Verri was rather critical (see note 2, p. 7 above) because the first was one of their administrator-heroes while the second was one of their villains in economic policy. For an interesting English comparative study of these two French finance ministers (and of Turgot, their counterpart in the eighteenth century) see Eleanor C. Lodge, Sully, Colbert, Turgot: A Chapter in French Economic History, London, Methuen, 1931.

this I add, that the more enlightened a people are, the surer the ruler will be that the ministers are working for the good of the State; for even if the authorities do not instinctively seek the public good, which is also the good of the ruler, they will be obliged to perform effectively according as the eyes of the people are opened, and as they are acute and intelligent observers of the conduct of the authorities. Therefore, *promotion of discernment and curiosity in matters of trade and finance* will always be the best preparation of all for initiating reforms.

XXXVI. WHETHER TAXATION AS SUCH IS USEFUL OR HARMFUL

Once the apportionment of taxation has been corrected, and it is reduced to the simplicity of two single parts; once domestic circulation is thus facilitated and transportation made free, and all coercive restraints on industry are removed, so that the people live by laws that are clear, simple, humane and inviolable; and once free rein is given to good faith, protected with all possible vigilance, there is no doubt that the nation will be seen to progress towards general well being. But, it may be asked, is a properly apportioned tax beneficial to national industry? Some writers[66] who believed this was so, relied on the following principle: tax makes the people poorer, hence it increases their wants, and therefore gives them added incentive to become industrious. It seems to me that another line of reasoning can be set against this, and this is as follows: tax removes a considerable portion of universal commodity from circulation for a period of time; therefore the circulation is reduced, and industry along [251] with it, because where the means of satisfying wants are reduced, they will be curbed; and as they diminish, the number of transactions will immediately fall, as we have several times stated;[67] and when transactions decrease, slower circulation will result. Furthermore, taxation is a reduction in the profit produced by industry; hence people will have less incentive to be industrious. Some have

---

[66] Among authors who subscribed to this philosophy and were familiar to Verri, the following may be mentioned: Sir Josiah Child, *A Discourse of Trade*, London, 1690, pp. 15-16; Bernard de Mandeville, *The Fable of the Bees*, London, 1714, pp. 173-74; Quesnay, "Grains" translated in Meek, *The Economics of Physiocracy*, p. 86; Hume, "Of Taxes," *Essays Moral, Political and Literary*, pp. 356-57.

[67] See for example, sections XIII, XIV, XVII and XXX, pp. 42-4, 47, 52-6, 92-4.

remarked,[68] that in the most prosperous cities heavier taxes are paid, and they almost seem to attribute prosperity to this fact, when on the contrary it is because of this [prosperity] that the heavy taxes can be tolerated without harm. If a bad transaction or activity in a nation with vigorous and widespread industry sometimes produces no apparent ill effects, this happens because large masses of solidly compacted matter, once heated, lose their heat slowly. The smaller a State is, the easier it is to revive it, or, conversely, to bring it to ruin. The larger the mass of men becomes, the greater the amount of time and the incentive needed to spur it on towards either good or evil.

A most attractive picture can be painted, to convince people that taxation is a good thing. Let us look at the countries of the world in general: we will see that those with a mild climate, those made most fertile by the sun, are inhabited by poor nations, largely inactive and barely acquainted with industry; conversely, the less productive climes, if they do not remain deserted, are inhabited by wealthy nations and highly industrious peoples. Extremes of cold are needed for man to use his invention in creating pleasant dwellings in which an air of the purest mildness may be breathed in the bitter depths of winter. It needs the sea to rise, threatening to submerge a country, for the land to become the most fertile garden in the world, rich with exotic plants. If you put a people on bare rock under threat of constant hunger, you will see them become the richest and most prolific producers in that part of the world. The tyrannical voice of need places men in a position of having either to perish or to become industrious; practice always goes beyond needs, and thus luxury and pleasures will rule that very soil where nature had planted death. Taxes have the same effect as sterility; for if a field cultivated by ten men in a fertile country produces [252] sufficient each year to feed thirty people, the owner of the land will be left with nourishment sufficient for twenty men whom he could employ, and this will be his revenue; in the same area of land in an unproductive climate, the work of ten men will produce sufficient to support twenty people, and there the owner will only obtain from it enough to maintain ten men. But if in the fertile area a tax is imposed, which makes the owner of the land pay half his income, he will be left with

---

[68] Perhaps a further reference to Hume "Of Taxes," *Essays Moral, Political and Literary*, pp. 356-57 who suggests such a possibility.

only sufficient to maintain ten men. The effect of the tax on land, therefore, in relation to the owner, is the same as the effect of the original unproductiveness of the soil. Therefore, some say that if the original unproductiveness spurs man on to industry, the same effect will be obtained by the artificial unproductiveness resulting from taxation.

But this manner of reasoning does not stand up, because one factor is missing. Man more readily perceives physical boundaries that do not change, than the changing and fluctuating limits represented by the thinking of those who govern him. Long experience, handed down to him by tradition, teaches him which physical obstacles he must overcome in order to go on living on a particular piece of land, which even though sterile is dear to him, because he was born there; he measures his strength against the obstacles, and knows that with just so much work he can overcome them, and may thereafter safely enjoy the fruits of his labour. But when the unproductiveness is artificial, what he sees is a hated obstacle which may grow larger the greater the effort he makes to overcome it. He becomes discouraged under the burden placed upon him, his trust in those who control his destiny diminishes, and he succumbs to indolence.

Thus I believe that, in general, taxation is always a diminution of industry, with the sole exception of a few timely duties imposed on the entry or exit of certain goods; in which case it can be of positive benefit to industry. In order to see how tax is in general a reduction of industry, let us go back to those principles of which something has been said elsewhere.[69] If in a given country no tax were to be paid, and some government organization were necessary to maintain the community, then in the advent [253] of unjust treatment or threat of invasion from some other country, it would be necessary for some portion of the people to abandon cultivation and manufacture, take up arms and hasten to the public defence, while the rest of the community remained occupied with annual reproduction for its own maintenance and that of its defenders. In this case, there can be no doubt that local industry and annual reproduction would be reduced, by an amount equivalent to the labour which was removed from cultivation and manufacture and transferred to the public defence. Instead of this, rather than removing the workers from agriculture and manufactures in time of need, men have been recruited whose

---

[69] Above, section XXIX, pp. 82-5.

profession it is to devote themselves entirely to the defence of the State, and instead of directly forwarding that part of the produce and commodities necessary for the nourishment of these defenders, the owners of those items exchange them for universal commodity, which they give to the treasury for the sustenance of the defenders. Thus the effect in both cases will be the same: that is to say, industry would be far greater and annual reproduction higher, if it were possible to achieve the vision of abolishing all taxes, as that most stupid and cruel of men who dishonored the throne of Augustus dared to propose to the Senate of Rome.[70]

A tax will always be less harmful in proportion to the speed with which it passes from the hands of the taxpayer into public funds, and from there to employees or public works; for then, even though this gives false momentum to a portion of the money in circulation, it will be returned to commerce in the shortest possible interval of time, to increase transactions, and the tax will be more harmless according as it is circulated in the same area from which it came, and the greater the number of people who share it when it comes out of the treasury.

XXXVII. OF THE SPIRIT OF FINANCE AND PUBLIC ECONOMY [254]

It is an observation worth making, that the principles which must animate a finance minister are largely different from those which must move the minister of public economy. If finance laws are *indirect*, they are useless; the laws of public economy, on the other hand, are useless if they are *direct* laws. Let me explain. In finance,

---

[70] A reference to Nero, presumably based on the following passage in Tacitus, *Annals of Rome*, Book XIII chapter 48 (A.D. 58).

> In this year there were persistent public complaints against the companies farming indirect taxes from the government. Nero contemplated a noble gift to the human race: he would abolish every indirect tax. But the senators whom he consulted, after loudly praising his noble generosity, restrained his impulse. They indicated that the empire could not survive without its revenues, and that abolition of the indirect customs dues would be followed by demands to abolish taxation also. Many companies for collecting indirect taxes, they recalled had been established by consuls and tribunes in the freest times of the Republic; since then such taxation had formed part of the efforts to balance income and expenditure. But Nero's advisers agreed that tax-collectors' acquisitiveness must be restrained, to prevent novel grievances from discrediting taxes long endured uncomplainingly.

(Translated by Michael Grant, Penguin Books, revised edition, 1977, pp. 308-9).

if a tax is collected under indirect laws, as for example if all citizens are forbidden to do something, not because it is in fact desired to prevent them from doing it, but so that they will buy an exemption to do it (and in many countries there are such laws); I say that this indirect tax will cost the nation a good deal more than the treasury will get out of it, and will often give rise to venality and corruption and time wasted in procuring favors. Thus the tax would be far more naturally and acceptably levied if the law of finance were clearly and directly to order payment of an equivalent sum on taxable land. If we study all the cases where a tax is indirect, we will discover that those many writers who find this form always defective are right.[71] Financial authorities must always go simply and openly to seek taxes from the taxpayer. Finance advances in a direct way towards its goals.

Public economy, however, must always move indirectly. The object of finance is to place as few constraints as possible on the nation in the imposition of taxation, the object of public economy is to raise annual reproduction to the highest possible level.[72] In finance there must be more authority and activity; public economy requires more shrewdness and delicacy. A few examples will clearly illustrate my ideas. Let us suppose we wish to increase the population of the State, spread cultivation to waste lands, and improve the nation's produce; I say that these provident notions would ruin a nation if they were promoted through direct laws, and if the lawgiver, instead of *invitation* and *guidance*, were to use force and *command*. [255] Examples of direct laws would be forbidding people to leave the State; making it compulsory for men to marry on reaching the age of twenty; ordering communities to put all the land in their district under cultivation; or laying down methods of preparation for silk, oil, and wine harvested from their land. The effects of these direct and restrictive laws would be depopulation and the devastation of the State. More and more people would leave, because men are less

---

[71] The major opponents of indirect taxation contemporary with Verri were the Physiocrats, whose views on this subject he here clearly supports. Hume, "Of Taxes," esp. pp. 356, 358, supported indirect taxes on commodities, where their invisibility for example, is favorably remarked on. As indicated in the introduction (above pp. xxiii-xxiv) much of Verri's material on taxation can be seen as a criticism of Hume. See above, pp. 108-9 and notes 66, 68.

[72] In 1769, in his *Riflessioni sulle leggi vincolanti* (pp. 288-89) Verri had defined the principle objective of public economy as obtaining the maximum annual reproduction possible, and proposed a ministry for this task with responsibilities very similar to those outlined in section XL (pp. 116-17 below).

content to remain in a place where they are constrained, than where they stay of their own free will; prisons would be full of wretched men guilty of no other crime than that of not betraying some young girl by associating her with their misery; communities would be exposed to intervention by the State if they did not cultivate land where manpower was lacking; hired soldiers and the dregs of society would shatter the sanctuary of people's homes to pry into the prescribed methods of preparation. In the midst of such internal chaos, confusion, disorder and despondency would spread everywhere, and the people in distress would take refuge in neighboring countries, looking for a new land where they might live their life tranquilly and be sure of enjoying it in peace as long as their hands remained clean of crime.

The prudent minister of public economy will move indirectly towards this end. Using honors and privilege, he will make the state of marriage respectable; he will revive industry by removing restraints, smoothing out roads and consolidating property, that most precious possession of social man, and by inducing in the people a deep conviction of their personal safety, for in this alone consists civil liberty; in short, he will release activity in the people by all those means we have seen, and as a result, population will increase, cultivation spread, and all the arts be refined.

XXXVIII. OF THE FIRST INCENTIVES TO REMEDY DISORDERS

We have seen what are the driving principles of industry, and what are the obstacles that hinder its development. Then we observed the methods that may be adopted by ministers to carry out beneficial reforms in a State. Finally, it remains for me to add an indication of how I believe the supreme arbiters of a society's destiny can set a beneficial revolution in progress. If human beings are ruled by habit above all else; if ancient customs, and the laws and usages handed down to us, in which we have been steeped since childhood, go to form the rules by which men live, this fact will be especially apparent in the tribunals. These, like immortal bodies movable only very slowly indeed from the line they follow, are the best custodians of the laws and systems of government from which order originates, and will embrace anything new only with the utmost difficulty. Each new individual brought in to sit on a tribunal will be forced to bow to the common way of thought, and the more venerable a tribunal is in the eyes of the people, the more each individual member, conscious of the honor of being part of it, will appropriate the opinions of the whole group and cherish them. No group of disparate people gathered together has ever been able either to carry out, or to attempt any reforms.

More heads, even in a new combination, are unlikely as a group to give expression to any new universal principle. Each individual, even supposing he has the most upright and impartial intentions, always has a private point of view from which he contemplates an issue; and just as several architects collectively will never produce a regular and uniform structure in any design, so neither, I believe, can a group of men acting as a tribunal ever organize a controlled system of reform. For if the passions, rivalries and preferences which sometimes enter men's hearts through human weaknesses [257] should become involved, the actions of those concerned will be wasted on anything but those matters immediately intended in the service of the ruler, that is to say for the good of the people; we see examples of this in history, and the internal affairs of many States bear witness to it. Wherever there has been some essential change, wherever with some speed and fortunate success old disorders have been rooted out, it will be seen that this was the work of one man alone, fighting against many private interests, which, if they had been obliged by majority vote to be subjected to individual debate, would have caused nothing but long and bitter wrangles. It therefore seems to me that in everything which has to do with the execution of existing laws it is useful, nay indispensable, for the decision to depend on the views of several men. Where, on the other hand, the concern is with organizing systems and steering a path towards a given goal, overcoming problems on the way which can never all be foreseen, this thrust and direction must of necessity depend on a single driving force, just as in Roman times a dictatorship was successfully adopted when things were difficult, whereas, when decemvirs were appointed, the results as we all know were unfortunate. When particular cases must be decided according to laws already issued, differences of opinion among men in fact make injustice unlikely to occur, because they are present at the same time; but when action is required to be prompt, expeditious and uniform towards a given end, I do not believe this can be made to depend on majority of votes.

Thus, in Political economy, and particularly when it needs to be simplified, involving the reform of old abuses, I say it is worthwhile to create a despotic system to last as long as is necessary to set in motion a provident system.

XXXIX. THE CHARACTERISTICS OF A MINISTER OF FINANCE

The belief that people fit jobs, rather than the reverse; an ability to resist favors in all forms; the capacity to acknowledge neither relatives, [258] nor friends nor clients; evaluating the service a chosen activity or transaction can render, not the person who has put it forward; a natural tendency to humble oneself as soon as the sacred voice of duty is heard; the ability to preserve in the midst of all this a humane and gentle attitude which will render the method of administering tax more acceptable to the public; a sincere desire for the success of the task in hand, with no thought of rivalry, and impartially seeking out what is true and useful; an ability to examine details thoroughly without losing sight of the main principles and the overall Picture; an intimate knowledge and conviction of the driving principles of industry; an analytical knowledge of the nature of man and society; a love of the good of the people in a spirit of true philanthropy; a precise knowledge of the condition of the country in which he must work; these are the qualities that would make a perfect man of finance, to whom a ruler could entrust the full authority necessary to establish a good system. But nature is not so generous with her gifts.[73]

The more enlightened people there are in a country, the greater the probability that the ruler will find a man resembling the character I have described. I need not add how necessary it is, that he be fully established and proven before he is given such extensive authority, and so great an influence on the public peace. Nor do I need to say how strong and consistent must be the ruler's protection of the person chosen, against whom there will be no lack of complaints and accusations in any country. In a time of reform, it is to be desired that everything proceed with the utmost dispatch and energy so that this period is as brief as possible and results in the organization of a smooth, yet regulated system with nothing arbitrary about it, and at that happy moment the power of man ceases and laws alone begin to rule once more. For men die, and systems remain, and men must not be chosen for positions as though everything had to rely on their prowess alone, nor must systems be set up as though nothing

---

[73] Verri's list of qualities required for a good minister of finance read similarly to those listed by Turgot in his "In Praise of Gournay" written on the occasion of the latter's death in 1759 (in *The Economics of A.R.J. Turgot*, edited P.D. Groenewegen, The Hague, Martinus Nijhoff, 1977, pp. 39-41).

depends on the virtues of the people chosen; and just as the need, [259] which the dictator was created to fill, ceased when Rome was content, and his authority was destroyed, so when the need no longer exists in the State, the rectified and simplified management of finance can be entrusted, if desired, to a group of several people, who will be custodians of a law which is already made and appropriate to the nation's interests.

I do not mean by this, to claim that this is the only means by which a corrupt financial system can be unequivocally remedied; there may be other methods arising out of particular conditions of countries and governments; I mean to say merely that a country in similar circumstances would do well to start on the road to progress using means not too dissimilar to those I have described.

XL. THE CHARACTERISTICS OF A MINISTER OF ECONOMY

I have indicated which qualities a minister of finance should have. From what I have said, it will also be apparent which talents a minister of economy ought to have. Above all, he must be active in destroying and most cautious in building. Most of the matters that concern him are inaccessible to the hand of man. Removal of obstacles, abolition of restrictions, smoothing the way to the competition that inspires reproduction, increasing civil liberty, leaving a wide field open to industry, protection of the reproducing class, in particular with good laws, so that the farmer or craftsman does not stand in fear of bullying by the rich; ensuring easy, rapid and disinterested movement in contracts of sale and purchase; spreading good faith in trade by never allowing fraud to go unpunished; fighting firmly and peacefully for the well understood cause of the people, which is, of course, always the cause of the ruler; never giving up hope of good, but hastening its coming by scattering the seeds of the most useful truths throughout the nation; these, and no others, are the matters which must concern a good minister of public economy. The rest must be left to the principle which is the direct driving force of the universe, and which [260] acts according to immutable laws, assembles all beings, and takes them apart, but does not lay waste nor leave anything idle, be it physical or political; a principle of which we see some effects, know the existence, admire the laws, and which we call by the vague and never defined term Nature. Happy is the man who cherishes this principle in his heart, and in obedience to the voice of the daughter of the All Powerful treads her path, and points it out to those who have lost it! Error and opinion alone hold men in chains, and lead entire nations to miserable unproductiveness.